Re-Reading the Eighteenth-Century Novel

Re-Reading the Eighteenth-Century Novel adds to the dynamically developing subfield of reception studies within eighteenth-century studies. Lipski shows how secondary visual and literary texts live their own lives in new contexts, while being also attentive to the possible ways in which these new lives may tell us more about the source texts. To this end the book offers five case studies of how canonical novels of the eighteenth century by Daniel Defoe, Henry Fielding and Laurence Sterne came to be interpreted by readers from different historical moments. Lipski prioritises responses that may seem non-standard or even disconnected from the original, appreciating difference as a gateway to unobvious territories, as well as expressing doubts regarding readings that verge on misinterpretative appropriation. The material encompasses textual and visual testimonies of reading, including book illustration, prints and drawings, personal documents, reviews, literary texts and literary criticism. The case studies are arranged in three sections: visual transvaluations, reception in Poland and critical afterlives, and are concluded by a discussion of the most recent socio-political uses and revisions of eighteenth-century fiction in the Age of Trump (2016–2020).

Jakub Lipski is associate professor and head of the Department of Anglophone Literatures at the Faculty of Literary Studies, Kazimierz Wielki University in Bydgoszcz. He is the author of *In Quest of the Self: Masquerade and Travel in the Eighteenth-Century Novel. Fielding, Smollett, Sterne* (2014) and *Painting the Novel: Pictorial Discourse in Eighteenth-Century English Fiction* (2018) as well as a number of articles and book chapters on eighteenth-century English literature. He has recently edited a collection of essays on the reception and afterlives of *Robinson Crusoe – Rewriting Crusoe: The Robinsonade Across Languages, Cultures, and Media* (2020).

Routledge Focus on Literature

Titles include:

Geomythology
How Common Stories are Related to Earth Events
Timothy J. Burbery

Re-Reading the Eighteenth-Century Novel
Studies in Reception
Jakub Lipski

Trump and Autobiography
Corporate Culture, Political Rhetoric, and Interpretation
Nicholas K. Mohlmann

Biofictions
Literary and Visual Imagination in the Age of Biotechnology
Lejla Kucukalic

Neurocognitive Interpretations of Australian Literature
Criticism in the Age of Neuroawareness
Jean-François Vernay

Mapping the Origins of Figurative Language in Comparative Literature
Richard Trim

Metaphors of Mental Illness in Graphic Medicine
Sweetha Saji & Sathyaraj Venkatesan

For more information about this series, please visit: https://www.routledge.com/Routledge-Focus-on-Literature/book-series/RFLT

Re-Reading the Eighteenth-Century Novel
Studies in Reception

Jakub Lipski

Routledge
Taylor & Francis Group

NEW YORK AND LONDON

First published 2021
by Routledge
605 Third Avenue, New York, NY 10158

and by Routledge
2 Park Square, Milton Park, Abingdon, Oxon OX14 4RN

Routledge is an imprint of the Taylor & Francis Group, an informa business

© 2021 Taylor & Francis

Library of Congress Cataloging-in-Publication Data
A catalog record for this title has been requested

ISBN: 978-0-367-71637-0 (hbk)
ISBN: 978-0-367-71638-7 (pbk)
ISBN: 978-1-003-15301-6 (ebk)

DOI: 10.4324/9781003153016

Typeset in Times New Roman
by Taylor & Francis Books

Contents

Figures

Acknowledgements

The five chapters constituting the core of this book are updated versions of the following essays:
"Poland's Finest Sternean: Izabela Czartoryska (1746–1835) as Reader and Promoter of Sterne". *The Shandean: an annual volume devoted to Laurence Sterne and his works* 27 (2016): 9–25. "Gothic Fielding? Philip James de Loutherbourg's *Tom Jones*". *Porównania. Czasopismo poświęcone zagadnieniom komparatystyki literackiej oraz studiom interdyscyplinarnym* 21 (2017): 259–267. "Sterne/Yorick, the sentimental traveller and contemporary travel writing studies: problematising the critical afterlife of *A Sentimental Journey*". *Porównania. Czasopismo poświęcone zagadnieniom komparatystyki literackiej oraz studiom interdyscyplinarnym* 24 (2019): 227–238. "Picturing Crusoe's Island: Defoe, Rousseau, Stothard". *Porównania. Czasopismo poświęcone zagadnieniom komparatystyki literackiej oraz studiom interdyscyplinarnym* 25 (2019): 85–99. "Setting the Scene for the Polish Robinsonade: *The Adventures of Mr. Nicholas Wisdom* (1776) by Ignacy Krasicki and the Early Reception of Robinson Crusoe in Poland, 1769–1775". In *Rewriting Crusoe: The Robinsonade across Languages, Cultures, and Media*, ed. Jakub Lipski. Lewisburg: Bucknell University Press, 2020, 52–64.

I would like to thank Emilia Kledzik, editor of *Porównania*, Peter de Voogd, editor of *The Shandean*, and Suzanne Guiod, director of Bucknell University Press, for allowing me to re-use this material.

I would also like to acknowledge my debts to Daniel Cook, Joanna Maciulewicz, Mary Newbould and the late Blake Gerard, as well as the two anonymous readers for Routledge. If their expert advice did not make this a better book, I am the only one to blame.

Introduction

When reception studies were gathering momentum as a refreshing alternative to text-oriented formalisms, Hans Robert Jauss famously asserted:

> A literary work is not an object that stands by itself and that offers the same view to each reader in each period. It is not a monument that monologically reveals its timeless essence. It is much more like an orchestration that strikes ever new resonances among its readers and that frees the text from the material of the words.[1]

The German critic challenged the New Critical belief in the "timelessness" of literary works and the passive role of readers as decoders of the never-changing, monological message imparted by the author. Paradoxically, he argued for the liberation of literature from "the material of the words"; nonsensical at first glance, this separation of literature from literariness is a metaphorical gesture of appreciation towards the reader – now an agent, too, in the literary-historical process.

Jauss's project was to re-establish literary history as a dominant way of talking about literature. His idea of literary history, however, was, in a sense, future oriented:

> A literary event can continue to have an effect only if those who come after it still or once again respond to it – if there are readers who again appropriate the past work or authors who want to imitate, outdo, or refute it.[2]

In other words, literary historians, however attentive they may be to the historical moment that produced the studied text, will discern only part of the story unless they place equal emphasis on the ways the text was read by later generations of readers, coming from different cultural and historical backgrounds.

DOI: 10.4324/9781003153016-1

One crucial question regards the methodology of studying readers' responses. The very act of reading, an individual's experience and making sense of a text, is an elusive phenomenon, often beyond the grasp of empirical research. One way of gaining critical insight into this practice is to examine textual and artistic testimonies in the form of literary response texts, personal notes and correspondence, reviews, critical examinations, illustrations and similar material. Admittedly, in this case the research places emphasis not on the act of reading itself but on another aesthetic entity that could well be examined on its own merits, irrespective of the source text that generated the response. That said, the method advocated by Jauss, and the wider idea of literary history that he put forward, not only prioritises intertextual links between the source texts and readers' responses that take the form of other texts, but also assumes that by scrutinising these responses we may uncover new meanings in the source texts, even those that had not originally been anticipated by the author. Hence the understanding of literary communication as a dialogue between the author and the reader, where each party has a say, rather than as the author's monologue.

The major benefit of placing emphasis on readers' responses, then, is the possibility of re-reading the source texts through the reader's testimony, showing how the originary text may function in a new context. To a point, this potential new use might be taken as evidence of the source's aesthetic complexity. Writing about the continuous appeal of Shakespeare's *Hamlet*, Jan Kott famously stated that the play is like "a sponge [that] immediately absorbs all the problems of our time".[3] This apt metaphor indicates not only the text's adaptability to new realities, but also the fact that these new contexts become part of the text's substance. A sponge that does not absorb anything is empty or at least incomplete – inactivated, as it were. Jauss's fellow member of the Constance School of reader response criticism Wolfgang Iser, and their critical ancestor Roman Ingarden, would label these empty sponge holes as "gaps" to be filled in by the reader.[4] However, while Ingarden's and Iser's "transactional" theories assume that gaps are programmed by the author and suggest specific responses within the designed structure of the text – the implied act of reading, Jauss's concept of the "horizon of expectations" goes beyond the individual reader's responses and recognises the phenomenon of what we would now term "collective" responses: the typical manners of reading at varying historical moments.[5]

This book adds to the dynamically developing subfield of reception studies within eighteenth-century studies. The most recent volumes of the burgeoning book series *The Reception of British and Irish Authors in Europe* (Bloomsbury) have explored figures from across the long eighteenth century as diverse as Isaac Newton, William Blake, and Edmund Burke.[6] Laurence Sterne's reception, and the role that adaptations of his fiction played within it, has proved to be an ongoing focus for critical work.[7] The afterlives of Aphra Behn, Jonathan Swift and Samuel Richardson have also received substantial attention,[8] let alone Jane Austen and Walter Scott, who fall beyond the scope of this book.[9] The 2019 *Robinson Crusoe* tercentenary, in turn, saw a heightened scholarly interest in the Robinsonade phenomenon, showing how this novel has successfully been colonising the popular imaginary for over 300 years, and how eighteenth-century material may remain topical and resonate with the here and now.[10] The visual and audio-visual reception of the early novel has also proved to be a vibrant field of critical insight, with studies engaging, among other things, with book illustration, painting, cinema and television.[11]

The Afterlives of Eighteenth-Century Fiction (2015, eds. Nicholas Seager and Daniel Cook), alongside a number of compelling case studies, foregrounds some crucial concepts enabling a better understanding of reception and adaptation processes. One of those is the notion of "afterlife", which implies that creative reception is not a passive process and that the new artistic entity generated by a source text merits attention as an autonomous work of art. "Afterlives" are also "lives made anew",[12] which brings us back to the notion of text as possessing a potential that can be continually *activated* in new contexts. The other central concepts problematised in this collection are those revolving around the notion of authorship, such as secondary authorship, appropriation, attribution and misattribution.[13] They question or complicate traditional critical agendas reconstructing patterns of influence and investigating the formal aspects of adaptation, and advocate instead a new literary history in which secondary texts write their own stories. As Cook and Seager put it, the volume's case studies are all based on "the conviction that where a text goes and by whom it is received matters as much as whence it originated".[14] This assumption is all the more accurate as regards eighteenth-century cultural production, given the fluid notions of intellectual property and originality in this period, as well as "the widespread resistance to closure in major and minor works of fiction".[15] Cook and Seager point out that in eighteenth-century literary and publishing practices "imitative writing was as valuable (in every sense) as 'original' work".[16] Accordingly, my general assumption throughout this book is that secondary visual and literary texts can not only live their own autonomous lives, beyond the "tyranny of the original",[17] but also tell us more about the source texts themselves.

To this end I offer five case studies of how canonical novels of the eighteenth century came to be interpreted by readers from different historical moments, as reflected by secondary cultural texts. I prioritise responses that may seem non-standard or even disconnected from the source text, appreciating difference as a gateway to unobvious territories, as well as expressing doubts regarding readings that verge on misinterpretative appropriation. My material encompasses textual and visual testimonies of reading, including book illustration, prints and drawings, personal documents, reviews, literary response texts, pieces of literary criticism, as well as popular and political newspaper articles. These case studies are arranged in three sections: visual transvaluations, reception in Poland and critical afterlives.

The readings of visual interpretations in Chapters 1 and 2 are informed by Gérard Genette's notion of transvaluation, discussed as a type of hypertextual relationship in his *Palimpsests*. Hypertextuality is one of Genette's basic realisations of transtextuality. He defines hypertextuality as "any relationship uniting a text B (... *hypertext*) to an earlier text A (... *hypotext*), upon which it is grafted in a manner that is not that of commentary".[18] As Genette explains, transvaluation involves two interpretative processes: devaluation and (counter)valuation;[19] that is, as some of the aspects of the hypotext's original value system are minimised, the hypertext puts emphasis elsewhere, thus promoting a different set of values, which may but does not have to become a form of counter-writing. Genette remarks that transvaluation often leads to a generic shift: the transformed system of values impinges on the hypertext's generic constitution. My approaches towards selected illustrations of Daniel Defoe's *Robinson Crusoe* (1719) and Henry Fielding's *Tom Jones* (1749) will show how the value and aesthetic systems of the original texts were negotiated once the fashion for realist representation gave way to the sentimental and the Gothic, respectively. The illustrations discussed re-vision the original stories, constructing narratives that seem far from those designed by Defoe and Fielding. Be that as it may, they activate a potential layer of meaning; one that could play out when the moment was right – when readers *expected* the sentimental and the Gothic.

The two case studies that follow reconstruct the dominant reception patterns of Laurence Sterne's work and Defoe's *Robinson Crusoe* in late eighteenth-century Poland. They exemplify micro-scale and macro-scale examinations, respectively. The chapter on Sterne involves focused readings of Princess Izabela Czartoryska's personal documents, which foreground her prominent role in orienting the reception of Sterne in Poland. The chapter on Defoe prioritises breadth rather than depth and reconstructs the main patterns of adopting and adapting Defoe's novel in Enlightenment Poland. Both chapters conclude by observing that the Sterne and the Defoe received in Poland might have been different from the original, but this adds further to this book's interest in negotiated meanings in new contexts. While serious reservations have been voiced against national reception studies,[20] with doubts expressed as to whether such investigations provide any insight into the source text at all, my belief throughout is that however distanced or disconnected from the source text these responses may seem to be, they play a role in the literary-historical process of on-going activations of the source text's potential against varying backgrounds of changing expectations.

In the "Critical afterlives" section I move from negotiated meanings to critical appropriation or misinterpretation. In a metacritical discussion of Sterne's *A Sentimental Journey* in Chapter 5 I address two critical topoi in contemporary travel writing studies: Laurence Sterne's agency in the so-called paradigm shift from the scientific to the subjective in eighteenth-century travel writing and the vague concept of "Sternean/Shandean fashions", which has tended to be used as an umbrella term for stylistic idiosyncrasies in post-1768 travel books. The former is approached as reflective of a style of reception that yearns to establish a myth of origin at the cost of historical accuracy. The latter is analysed with reference to the East Central European notion of *sternizm*, and exemplifies a pattern of disconnection, where a critical term derived from a name begins an autonomous life of its own and loses contact with the point of origin. The ensuing Coda completes this section, as well as concluding the book as a whole, by offering insight into the most recent uses of eighteenth-century fiction in socio-political contexts against the background of the so-called Age of Trump (2016–2020). In evaluating the potential of *Robinson Crusoe*, Jonathan Swift's *Gulliver's Travels*, Samuel Richardson's *Pamela* and Olaudah Equiano's *The Interesting Narrative* to respond to the topical issues of the here and now, I draw on material that ranges from political newspaper articles to satirical cartoons to ponder the more general question of why to read the eighteenth-century novel today.[21]

Collectively, the case studies illustrate the diverse possibilities for literary texts to live their afterlives in varying historical moments. No attempt is made here at comprehensiveness: indeed, just as reception itself is an on-going and open-ended process, so is critical writing about the phenomenon. The loose, case-based structure of what follows, I believe, is the only reasonable way to approach this vast field, as any totalising argumentative trajectories will inevitably give the impression of arbitrariness and artificial ordering. My emphasis on canonical texts by such old familiars as Daniel Defoe, Jonathan Swift, Samuel Richardson, Henry Fielding and Laurence Sterne is – I hope – balanced by secondary texts, some of which are rather obscure and will be unknown to the reader. Focused discussions of formal and aesthetic issues, in turn, are juxtaposed with factual chapters, reconstructing specific historical moments of reception. Indeed, a book on reading patterns and strategies should manifest an openness to various readerly expectations, and it is my hope that the following case studies will find their audience(s).

Notes

1 Hans Robert Jauss, *Toward an Aesthetic of Reception* (Minneapolis: University of Minnesota Press, 1982), 21.
2 Jauss, *Toward an Aesthetic of Reception*, 22.
3 Jan Kott, *Shakespeare Our Contemporary*, trans. Bolesław Taborski (New York: Double Day, 1964), 84.
4 See Wolfgang Iser, *The Act of Reading: A Theory of Aesthetic Response* (London: Routledge & Kegan Paul, 1978), 180–202.
5 See Jauss, *Toward an Aesthetic of Reception*, 88–89.
6 See Helmut Pulte and Scott Mandelbrote (eds.), *The Reception of Isaac Newton in Europe* (London: Bloomsbury, 2019); Morton D. Paley and Sibylle Erle (eds.), *The Reception of William Blake in Europe* (London: Bloomsbury, 2019); Martin Fitzpatrick and Peter Jones (eds.), *The Reception of Edmund Burke in Europe* (London: Bloomsbury, 2017).
7 See Peter de Voogd and John Neubauer (eds.), *The Reception of Laurence Sterne in Europe* (London: Continuum, 2004), M-C. Newbould, *Adaptations of Laurence Sterne's Fiction: Sterneana, 1760–1840* (Aldershot and Burlington: Ashgate, 2013) and the numerous focused studies published in Sterne journal *The Shandean*.
8 See, for example, Jane Spencer, *Aphra Behn's Afterlife* (Oxford: Oxford University Press, 2000); David A. Brewer, *The Afterlife of Character, 1726–1825* (Philadelphia: University of Pennsylvania Press, 2005); Hermann J. Real (ed.), *The Reception of Jonathan Swift in Europe* (London: Continuum, 2005); Natasha Simonova, *Early Modern Authorship and Prose Continuations: Adaptation and Ownership from Sidney to Richardson* (Houndmills: Palgrave Macmillan, 2015).
9 See, for example, Anthony Mandal and Brian Southam (eds.), *The Reception of Jane Austen in Europe* (London: Continuum, 2007); Ann Rigney, *The Afterlives of Walter Scott: Memory on the Move* (Oxford: Oxford University Press, 2012).
10 See, for example, Ian Kinane (ed.), *Didactics and the Modern Robinsonade* (Liverpool: Liverpool University Press, 2019); Jakub Lipski (ed.), *Rewriting Crusoe: The Robinsonade across Languages, Cultures, and Media* (Lewisburg: Bucknell University Press, 2020); Andreas K E Mueller and Glynis Ridley (eds.), *Robinson Crusoe after 300 Years* (Lewisburg: Bucknell University Press, 2021); and Emmanuelle Peraldo (ed.), *300 Years of Robinsonades* (Newcastle: Cambridge Scholars, 2020).
11 See, for example, Christina Ionescu and Ann Lewis (eds.), Special Issue: *Picturing the Eighteenth-Century Novel through Time: Illustration, Intermediality and Adaptation, Journal for Eighteenth-Century Studies* 39.4 (2016); Catherine M. Gordon, *British Paintings of Subjects from the English Novel, 1740–1870* (New York: Garland, 1988); Robert Mayer (ed.), *Eighteenth-Century Fiction on Screen* (Cambridge: Cambridge University Press, 2002); Karen Bloom

Gevirtz, *Representing the Eighteenth-Century in Film and Television, 2000–2015* (Houndmills: Palgrave Macmillan, 2017).

12 Anna Holland and Richard Scholar (eds.), *Pre-Histories and Afterlives: Studies in Critical Method for Terence Cave* (London: Legenda, 2009) after Daniel Cook and Nicholas Seager, "Introduction", in *The Afterlives of Eighteenth-Century Fiction*, ed. Daniel Cook and Nicholas Seager (Cambridge: Cambridge University Press, 2015), 2.

13 See Daniel Cook, "On Authorship, Appropriation, and Eighteenth-Century Fiction", in *The Afterlives of Eighteenth-Century Fiction*, ed. Cook and Seager, 20–42.

14 Cook and Seager, "Introduction", 16.

15 Cook, "On Authorship, Appropriation, and Eighteenth-Century Fiction", 22.

16 Cook and Seager, "Introduction", 14.

17 Cook and Seager, "Introduction", 5.

18 Gérard Genette, *Palimpsests: Literature in the Second Degree*, trans. Channa Newman and Claude Doubinsky (Lincoln and London: University of Nebraska Press, 1997), 5.

19 Genette, *Palimpsests*, 367.

20 See numerous *Scriblerian* reviews by Melvyn New.

21 Since reception and afterlives are the focus here, I do not approach the more formal issues of genre. The understanding of "novel" in what follows is rather broad, inclusive of such texts as Swift's *Gulliver's Travels* and Equiano's *Interesting Narrative*, which in more formally oriented studies of the "rise" of the eighteenth-century novel are not considered as novels proper.

Part I
Visual Transvaluations

1 Re-Visioning Robinson's Island

Thomas Stothard's Rousseauvian *Crusoe*

At the beginning of J. M. Coetzee's *Foe* (1986), we read:

> For readers reared on travellers' tales, the words *desert isle* may
> conjure up a place of soft sands and shady trees where brooks run
> to quench the castaway's thirst and ripe fruit falls into his hand,
> where no more is asked of him than to drowse the days away till a
> ship calls to fetch him home. But the island on which I was cast
> away was quite another place.[1]

Susan Barton, the female castaway of Coetzee's novel, proceeds to offer a
very detailed sketch of the island, presenting it as a hostile and by no
means picturesque environment; an impression that is created by such
details as "drab bushes", "swarms of large pale fleas" and rocks "white
with [birds'] droppings".[2] This pictorial moment is introduced by way of
evoking the typical expectations of a desert island the reader might have
and then negating them, very much in line with the poetics of counter-
canonical writing that *Foe*, at least to a certain degree, follows. But the
paradise-like setting referred to by Susan Barton is a construct that does
not go back to Daniel Defoe's *Robinson Crusoe*; rather, it is a product of a
significant transformation in the way the environment of the island was
depicted in the eighteenth-century Robinsonade.[3] My aim in this chapter
will be to reconstruct some of the fundamental steps in this process.

Defoe's Island

Defoe's interest in painting and his use of pictorialism in narrative prose
have already been given substantial critical attention.[4] In sum, while the
author of *Crusoe* would not deserve the credit of a Dickensian stylist, he
was able to include well-developed pictorial passages in his prose fiction
that as a rule drew attention to crucial ideological and narrative

DOI: 10.4324/9781003153016-3

moments.[5] These include the memorable portrait of Roxana in her Turkish dress in *Roxana* (1724), illustrative of her protean identity and social ascension, or the first meeting with Friday in *Robinson Crusoe* (1719), constituting the core of *Crusoe*'s imperialist iconography.

In the island section of the first volume of *Robinson Crusoe*, there are several scenes rendered in pictorial terms, which prompted the formation of what might be termed the Robinsonade iconography: Robinson's reaction on the shore, when he is "making a thousand gestures and motions which [he] cannot describe" (91);[6] Robinson and his "family", concluding the survival narrative of the island section (166); Robinson sketching his appearance (167–168); Robinson describing his "Plantations" and "Fortifications" (169); Robinson and the footprint, with the memorable indication of stasis – "I stood like one Thunder-struck" (170); Robinson in his cave-magazine (188–189), which Maximillian Novak has analysed with reference to the iconography of eremite saints;[7] Robinson meeting Friday (207); and, finally, Robinson prepared for a battle with the English mutineers (245). In these, Defoe diversifies the writing in terms of length, level of details, objects described, but one thing does not change – an apparent obliviousness to the beauties of nature.

There are moments in the early parts of the desert island section when Robinson is clearly observing his surroundings, but his interests lie in practicalities and everyday necessities:

> I began to look round me to see what kind of Place I was in, *and* what was next to be done ... (91) I look'd about me again, *and* the first thing I found was the Boat ... (92) My next Work was to view the Country, *and* seek a proper Place for my Habitation ... (96) (emphasis mine)

The parallel structure of the above – the repetitious use of "and" changing or specifying Robinson's interests – is indicative of a narrative pace in which there is no room for descriptive passages. This is indeed the case but only to a point. As mentioned before, Robinson does from time to time introduce narrative pauses to make space for detailed pictorial passages; landscaping is simply not his priority.

The strongest piece of evidence for Crusoe's insensitivity to natural scenery can be found when Robinson climbs a hill to view the environs (96–97). Again, there is little more that the reader learns from the account than the fact that the place is an island. Robinson is much more articulate on his use of rifles and first attempts at hunting. This is surprising, not least because of the fact that in the contemporaneous travel accounts literary landscapes tended to be introduced by travellers ascending a hill for the sake of a better view. The scene involves the reader's visual imagination: we concretise the island by imagining what it looks like to Robinson, the focaliser in this scene, while Robinson himself concentrates on the culinary prospects of the place. Needless to say, it was not untypical of later Robinsonades to rewrite the climbing of the hill scene and indeed provide relevant and much expected descriptions.

The perspective is reversed in another memorable pictorial moment, towards the end of the island section. This time the castaway braces himself for the upcoming encounter with visitors to *his* island. The scene would have inspired the frontispiece to the first edition of *Crusoe* (Figure 1.1), frequently reprinted, despite some differences between the sketch and the picture. The more developed portrait of Crusoe given earlier on, in turn, inspired the French illustrator Bernard Picart, who created the frontispiece for the first French edition published in 1720 (Figure 1.2). While there is nothing that we learn about the natural scenery constituting the background against which Crusoe poses, the two frontispieces include a bit of the island in the background.

Bibliographers and book historians, most notably Rodney Baine, have pointed out that Defoe himself had nothing to say as to the preliminaries of *Robinson Crusoe* and the other novels, including the frontispieces.[8] Nevertheless, contemporary print culture scholars, for example Janine Barchas, have persuasively demonstrated how the paratext becomes a meaningful element of the text, despite the author's intentions or lack thereof.[9] In this sense, the frontispiece, as an important framing element, functions as a "threshold of interpretation", to use Gérard Genette's words.[10] The island as depicted in the frontispieces provides a lens through which the reader can view its presence in the actual narrative. The visible palisade, an element of Robinson's fortifications, foregrounds the idea of enclosure, possession and conquest over the natural world, thus corresponding to Crusoe's shifting attention, from the presence of the surrounding wilderness to his own survival and civilising ventures. This use of the natural world is central to *Robinson Crusoe* throughout the narrative, and it even prompted Novak to argue that conquest of nature should be regarded as a determinative element of the Robinsonade as a genre, distinguishing it from other types of desert island fiction.[11]

In the early 1720s, Defoe started producing his monumental *Tour Thro' the Whole Island of Great Britain*. The account features a number of pictorial passages, including ones describing estate gardens, seemingly centring on the beauties of landscape. One of those is a passage devoted to Sir Richard Child's, "the most delicious as well as most spacious pieces of Ground for Gardens that is to be seen in all this part of England":[12]

Figure 1.1 Frontispiece to the first edition of *Robinson Crusoe*. 1719. Hathi-Trust Digital Library.

Figure 1.2 Bernard Picart, Frontispiece to the first French edition of *Robinson Crusoe*. 1720. Beinecke Digital Collections.

As the Front of the House opens to a long row of Trees, reaching to the Great Road at *Leighton Stone*; so the Back-Face, or Front, *if that be proper*, respects the Gardens, and with an easy Descent lands you

upon the Terras, from whence is a most Beautiful Prospect to the
River, which is all form'd into Canals and Openings, to answer the
Views from above, and beyond the River, the Walks and Wildernesses
go on to such a Distance, and in such a manner up the Hill, as they
before went down, that the Sight is lost in the Woods adjoining, and
it looks all like one planted Garden as far as the Eye can see.[13]

Defoe is still faithful to the classical ideal of nature controlled; he
praises the *art* of landscaping, rather than landscapes themselves: ter-
races, canals, walks, openings. As if that were not enough, the spatial
design fools the eye so that the actual "Woods adjoining" look like a
"planted Garden", indicating effects of human agency.

Arguably, this excerpt helps better to understand the one passage in
Robison Crusoe, where natural description comes forcefully to the fore, that
is, when Crusoe marvels at the "delicious Vale" that will later serve as the
background of his "Country-House": "the Country appear'd so fresh, so
green, so flourishing, every thing being in constant Verdure, or Flourish of
Spring, that it looked like a planted Garden" (131). The similar diction
used in these two pictorial moments, as well as the immediate context in the
novel – "to think that this was all my own, that I was King and Lord of all
this Country" (131) – shows that natural beauty in *Crusoe* is appreciated
when the island becomes the king-castaway's possession and estate. As
Novak aptly puts it, Robinson's "Eden ... is to be part of what every English gentleman might wish to claim as his right".[14]

Rousseau's Transvaluation

To Crusoe, the island becomes a positively evaluated space only when
contrasted with the dangers elsewhere or when serving a specific narrative and ideological function – of Crusoe's kingdom. A fuller appreciation of the natural beauties of the island for their own merits takes
place in the second half of the century, especially following a new
reading of Defoe's text offered by J. J. Rousseau.[15] This brings Crusoe's
island closer to the ideals of a sentimental, and later Romantic, delight
in the natural world, a tradition that stems from mythological visuali-
sations of the island as a paradise regained, as represented in Antoine
Watteau's series of paintings *Pilgrimage to Cythera* (Figure 1.3) and
later eighteenth-century rococo iconography (Figure 1.4).

Before addressing Rousseau himself, I would like to quote a seemingly unrelated passage from August Fryderyk Moszyński's *Essay sur
le jardinage Anglois* (1774), which the author – the last Polish King
Stanislaus's architect and adviser – presented to the monarch. Among

Figure 1.3 Nicolas Henri Tardieu, after Antoine Watteau, "The Embarkation for Cythera", 1733. G3821. Harvard Art Museums/Fogg Museum. Gift of William Gray from the collection of Francis Calley Gray. Photo © President and Fellows of Harvard College.

the several dozen recommended embellishments, "Robinson Crusoe's habitation" is described as a fashionable addition to the Royal Gardens in Łazienki, Warsaw:

> The remnants of what used to be a path and the few fallen trees make one curious to delve into the forest. Having taken some turns through trees and bushes, the visitor reaches Robinson's habitation, just as it was described in the novel. The hut can be entered by an underground passage, and the interior corresponds to what it was like for Robinson. His tools are hung on the walls and serve as embellishments. A wooden palisade, masked by the brush from the outside, encloses and conceals the hut when one views it from the meadow located in this part of the forest. ... One can walk back taking the same path or turn right and go further into the forest to reach Trophonius' cave.[16]

There is no evidence that the proposed plan materialised, but the context of the neighbouring Trophonius's cave suggests that the idea of

Figure 1.4 Jean Jacques de Boissieu, "Wooded Island", 1763. The Metropolitan Museum of Art. Gift of Mrs Algernon S. Sullivan, 1919.

Robinson's hut as an element of garden design corresponded to other "caves", "grottos", "huts" or "hermitages" in picturesque gardens. As such, it is testimony to a sentimental reading of Defoe's novel, with the reader's focus centred on the relationship between the solitary individual and Nature – an ideal form of contact encouraged by the picturesque garden and the possibilities of spiritual retreat that it offered.

This ideal was promoted by J. J. Rousseau, and not only in his *Emile, or, On Education*, which is a typical reference point in studies of the Robinsonade (see Chapter 3), but also elsewhere. In fact, as Mary Bellhouse persuasively argues, when Rousseau reinterpreted the story of Crusoe, he separated two mythical aspects: the myth of a reunion with nature (constructed in *Confessions, The New Heloise* and *The Solitary Walker*) and the educational myth. As Bellhouse writes, the former was the ideal for Rousseau himself; the latter, for the social and political programme he promoted.[17] Descriptions of nature are, of course, prioritised in the former set of writings. For example, in *The New Heloise*, which influenced the changing fashions in garden design, St Preux (having himself spent some time on a desert island) compares the garden of Julie to the isle of Juan Fernandez, where Alexander Selkirk, the real-life model for Crusoe, was stranded:

> This place [Elysium], although quite close to the house, is so well hidden by the shaded avenue separating them that it cannot be seen from anywhere. ... Upon entering this so-called orchard, I was struck by a pleasantly cool sensation which dark shade, bright and lively greenery, flowers scattered on every side, the bubbling of flowing water, and the songs of a thousand birds impressed on my imagination at least as much as my senses; but at the same time I thought I was looking at the wildest, most solitary place in nature, and it seemed to me I was the first mortal who ever had set foot in this wilderness. Surprised, stunned, transported by a spectacle so unexpected, I remained motionless for a moment, and cried out in spontaneous ecstasy: O Tinian! O Juan Fernandez! Julie, the ends of the earth are at your gate![18]

A similar construct of the island as a new paradise, this time in the context of positively evaluated isolation, is given in Rousseau's *The Solitary Walker*:

> When the evening approached, I descended from the summits of the island, and I went gladly to sit down on the border of the lake, on the shore, in some hidden nook: there, the sound of the waves and the agitation of the water, fixing my senses and driving every other agitation from my soul, plunged it into a delicious reverie where the night often surprised me without reverie, my having perceived it. The flux and reflux of this water, its continual sound, swelling at intervals, struck ceaselessly my ears and eyes, responding to the internal movements which the reverie extinguished in me, and sufficed to make me feel my existence with pleasure, without taking the trouble to think.[19]

Stothard's Rousseauvian *Crusoe*

Rousseau's appreciation of *Robinson Crusoe* revived and reoriented the interest in the myth of Robinson, especially on the Continent (see Chapter 3). That said, in Britain, after the initial surge of editions, there was an observable slowdown in the mid-century decades, and what renewed the interest in Defoe and *Crusoe* was the 1781 edition, included in James Harrison's series *The Novelist's Magazine*, which contained seven drawings by the renowned illustrator Thomas Stothard.[20] This was the first major illustration project for *Robinson Crusoe* after the early editions, and the change in artistic quality is striking. This gave way to the 1790 edition by John Stockdale, which included fourteen illustrations by Stothard. As David Blewett points out, in contrast to the relatively random set for the 1781 edition, these constituted an autonomous narrative programme "very much in the tradition of eighteenth-century narrative painting in the manner of Hogarth's well-known 'progresses'",[21] and as such have been regarded as "the first English pictorial treatment of Robinson Crusoe as a progress",[22] beginning with Crusoe, here considerably younger, taking his leave of his parents.

Blewett argues that Stothard's pieces bring Defoe's novel closer to Rousseau's thought system, though he focuses on the representation of Friday (Figure 1.5) and the concepts of the noble savage and state of nature.[23] In this, the illustrator elaborated on what is present not only in Rousseau's interpretation, but also in Defoe's novel itself: let us recall the sketch of Friday's figure, foregrounding his "Sweetness and Softness", and Crusoe's discussion of the natural predisposition for correct judgement that comes shortly after (209, 212). Pointing to the muscular torso of Friday, Blewett recognises Stothard's use of Raphael's aesthetic.[24] That being clearly the case, I would like to draw attention to the other aspect of Stothard's Rousseauvian interpretation, which, rather than elaborating on an aspect of Defoe's novel, compensates for a meaningful omission: the beauties of nature. If the foregrounding of the naturally noble Friday may be taken as a response to the socio-educational myth promoted by Rousseau, the greater attentiveness to the natural world should be seen as elaborating on the myth of back to nature. I would argue that in Stothard's illustrations the mythical dimension of the back to nature narrative is reflected in a twofold manner: literally, by way of reconstructing the natural world in a more attractive and detailed manner; and metaphorically, by implying the dominance of the environment and man's reunion with Mother Nature.

The idea that seems to be displayed by the majority of Stothard's illustrations is that of nature welcoming and encompassing Crusoe rather than being conquered by him. The natural environs, for the most part, are presented as if from the inside; they are certainly beyond the colonising grasp of the castaway, and create the illusion of a three-dimensional space in which the character is immersed, rather than being represented as a flat surface to be written over by demarcating lines. Stothard's Crusoe does not seem to need "three or four Compasses, some Mathematical Instruments, Dials, Perspectives, Charts, and Book of Navigation" (105), instruments that in Defoe's novel indicate a scientific perspective on the island as a space of colonial exploration and conquest. In a sense, Stothard's Crusoe is healed of what Robert Marzec labels "the Crusoe

Figure 1.5 C. Heath, after Thomas Stothard, "Robinson Crusoe first sees and
rescues his man Friday". From John Stockdale's 1790 edition of
Robinson Crusoe. The Victorian Web. Photo: Philip V. Allingham.

syndrome" – that is, "the terror of inhabiting the other space *as* other ...
until the land is enclosed and transformed".[25]

This is best reflected in the two scenes that depict Crusoe's civilising
acts as no threat to the island: "Robinson Crusoe and Friday making a
boat" (Figure 1.6) and "Robinson Crusoe and Friday making a tent to

lodge Friday's father and the Spaniard" (Figure 1.7). In both illustrations the background dominates and encompasses the human figures. The diagonal placement of the boat amplifies the illusion of three-dimensionality, while the contemplative countenance of Crusoe and his gentle stroke of the boat do not give the idea of a hard worker transforming the natural resources but rather of a pensive solitaire, maybe not even willing to leave the regained paradise. The making of the tent, in turn, foregrounds the idea of a harmonious co-existence. The tent itself is hardly visible and the focus is placed on one of the supporting poles that runs parallel to the surrounding trees. Phillip Allingham points out that Stothard emphasises here the motif of familial relations against a welcoming natural backdrop. As he writes, the scene shows "Europeans fitting into the natural environment rather than simply imposing their will upon it".[26]

The same strategy of designing the human forms in a way that would imply a blend of the characters and their natural backdrop is used in the already-mentioned illustration of Robinson rescuing Friday (Figure 1.5). The classical iconography of *figura serpentinata* is used here to emphasise the harmonious co-presence of man and nature, the serpentine postures of Robinson and Friday imitating as it were, the shapes of the bended trees. Stothard may have been applying the theoretical observations of William Hogarth, who argued in his *The Analysis of Beauty* that the waving line – the line of beauty – is derived from the world of nature and supported the argument with a number of examples ranging from trees and flowers to the human body, such as the following:

> Of these fine winding forms then are the muscles and bones of the human body composed, and which, by their varied situations with each other, become more intricately pleasing, and form a continued waving of winding forms from one into the other.[27]

Two of Stothard's engravings sketch a wider panorama of the island. In the scene showing Crusoe retrieving goods from the shipwreck (Figure 1.8), the background offers skilfully composed and sentimentally biased scenery, which, as Blewett argues, brings to mind the qualities of a "beautifully landscaped English park".[28] A similar idea seems to be conveyed by the scene of Crusoe in his cave (Figure 1.9), in which the opening displays a view very much in line with the way views were meant to present themselves through the windows of eighteenth-century country houses – an impression created by the framing of the cave's walls and the palisade, and the curtain drawn to the side.

The island then does become a familiar space, but this is not done through Crusoe's transformation of it; on the contrary, Stothard's

Figure 1.6 C. Heath, after Thomas Stothard, "Robinson Crusoe and Friday making a boat". From John Stockdale's 1790 edition of *Robinson Crusoe*. The Victorian Web. Photo: Philip V. Allingham.

landscaping implies an approval of the modern view on the garden as a space that should preserve or recreate the naturalness of the natural world.[29] Stothard's island is not a geographical spot for conquest, but an idealised background for Crusoe's moderately civilisational ventures, which – importantly – seem to be doing very little damage to the island as such. The myth of civilisation is not rendered here in terms that suggest a

Figure 1.7 C. Heath, after Thomas Stothard, "Robinson Crusoe and Friday
making a tent to lodge Friday's father and the Spaniard". From
John Stockdale's 1790 edition of *Robinson Crusoe*. The Victorian
Web. Photo: Philip V. Allingham.

thorough restructuring of the setting, as is indeed the case in Defoe's novel
and the early illustrations, but as a process of harmonious co-existence.

The final illustration that merits attention is the one directly alluding to
the previously mentioned frontispieces to the early editions of *Crusoe* in
English and French (Figure 1.10). Unlike its models from 1719 and 1720,

Figure 1.8 C. Heath, after Thomas Stothard, "Robinson Crusoe upon the raft". From John Stockdale's 1790 edition of *Robinson Crusoe*. The Victorian Web. Photo: Philip V. Allingham.

though, the background shows no human interference whatsoever. Crusoe's figure merges with it – an effect achieved by the engraver's use of the same technique for the castaway's outfit and the leaves of the trees behind him. Rather than showing how Robinson transformed the space, the scene seems to imply that the space transformed the man and gave birth to a new "natural" Crusoe.

Figure 1.9 C. Heath, after Thomas Stothard, "Robinson Crusoe at work in his cave". From John Stockdale's 1790 edition of *Robinson Crusoe*. The Victorian Web. Photo: Philip V. Allingham.

Even if not pictured in an extensive manner, the island in Defoe's novel is by all means given names: the labelling varies from "a horrible desolate Island", "this dismal unfortunate Island", and "the Island of Despair" to "this horrid Place", "this dreadful Place" and "Prison"; this negative evaluation changes in the course of the narrative as Crusoe redefines his

Figure 1.10 C. Heath, after Thomas Stothard, "Robinson Crusoe in his Island
dress". From John Stockdale's 1790 edition of *Robinson Crusoe*.
The Victorian Web. Photo: Philip V. Allingham.

condition in the context of God's Providence and asserts his authority on
the island, but even then, the changed perspective is offered when the conquered and homely island is juxtaposed with the dangers of the unknown at
sea or with Crusoe's recognition of himself as a coloniser and king. Seventy-
nine years later, Maria Edgeworth in *Practical Education* (1798) would

write "A desert island is a delightful place, to be equalled only by the skating land of the rein-deer, or by the valley of diamonds in the Arabian tales".[30] This is a major shift in evaluating the island setting, which proved highly influential for the Romantic Robinsonade in the early decades of the nineteenth century. This transvaluation goes back to sentimentalised readings of *Crusoe* and his island which were gathering momentum in the second half of the eighteenth century, aligning the Robinsonade poetics to the rococo iconography of islands as paradise regained.

Notes

Research for this chapter was facilitated by the Schwerpunkt Polen fellowship at the University of Mainz, June–July 2019. It is an updated and developed version of the following article: Jakub Lipski, "Picturing Crusoe's Island: Defoe, Rousseau, Stothard", *Porównania* 25 (2019): 85–99.

1 J.M. Coetzee, *Foe* (London: Penguin Books, 1987), 7.
2 Coetzee, *Foe*, 7–8.
3 Maximillian Novak argues that narratives of paradise islands, fictions of "a quest for a new paradise", are not strictly speaking Robinsonades, even if featuring a shipwreck. As Novak demonstrates, this narrative tradition was developing separately of the Robinsonade, especially in the seventeenth century, despite some obvious interrelations. Maximillian E. Novak, *Transformations, Ideology, and the Real in Defoe's* Robinson Crusoe *and Other Narratives: Finding "The Thing Itself"* (Newark: University of Delaware Press, 2015), Chapter 6: "Edenic Desires: *Robinson Crusoe*, the Robinsonade, and Utopian Forms", 111–127. Ian Kinane, in turn, approaches the Robinsonade as a genre that is invariably concerned with cultural projections of "paradise", both as a physical entity and a psychological concept. Ian Kinane, *Theorising Literary Islands: The Island Trope in Contemporary Robinsonade Narratives* (London and New York: Rowman & Littlefield International, 2017), Chapter 4: "Islands of Paradise?", 137–176.
4 See, especially, Novak, *Transformations, Ideology, and the Real in Defoe's* Robinson Crusoe *and Other Narratives*, 43–60.
5 My understanding of pictorialism in this chapter will be in line with the traditional definition put forward by Jean Hagstrum: "In order to be called 'pictorial', a description or an image must be, in its essentials, capable of *translation* into painting or some other visual art". Jean H. Hagstrum, *The Sister Arts: The Tradition of Literary Pictorialism and English Poetry from Dryden to Gray* (Chicago: University of Chicago Press, 1958), 20.
6 Parenthetical references to *Robinson Crusoe* use the following edition: Daniel Defoe, *The Life and Strange Surprising Adventures of Robinson Crusoe* (1719). *The Novels of Daniel Defoe*, ed. W. R. Owens and P. N. Furbank. Vol. 1 (London: Pickering & Chatto, 2008).
7 Novak, *Transformations, Ideology, and the Real in Defoe's* Robinson Crusoe *and Other Narratives*, 163.
8 Rodney M. Baine, "The Evidence from Defoe's Title Pages", *Studies in Bibliography* 25 (1972): 185.

9 Janine Barchas, *Graphic Design, Print Culture, and the Eighteenth-Century Novel* (Cambridge: Cambridge University Press, 2003), 5.
10 Gérard Genette, *Paratexts: Thresholds of Interpretation*, trans. Jane E. Lewin (Cambridge: Cambridge University Press, 1997).
11 Novak, *Transformations, Ideology, and the Real in Defoe's* Robinson Crusoe *and Other Narratives*, 112. Ilse Vickers offers an insightful analysis of this aspect of the Crusoe story with reference to the developing New Sciences. See the chapter "Robinson Crusoe: man's progressive dominion over nature", in Ilse Vickers, *Defoe and the New Sciences* (Cambridge: Cambridge University Press, 1996), 99–131.
12 Daniel Defoe, *Writings on Travel, Discovery and History*, ed. W. R. Owens and P. N. Furbank. Volume 1: *A Tour Thro' the Whole Island of Great Britain*, *volume I*, ed. John McVeagh (London: Pickering and Chatto, 2001–2002), 130.
13 Defoe, *A Tour...*, 131.
14 Novak, *Transformations, Ideology, and the Real in Defoe's* Robinson Crusoe *and Other Narratives*, 122.
15 Two notable examples preceding Rousseau and Robinsonades in his wake, and characterised by a greater sensitivity to the beauties of nature, are Peter Longueville's *The Hermit, or, the Unparalled Sufferings and Surprising Adventures of Mr Philip Quarll, an Englishman* (1727) and Robert Paltock's *The Life and Adventures of Peter Wilkins* (1751). The former abounds in enthusiastically sensuous passages, as in the following: "a Grass Carpet, imbroider'd with beautiful Flowers of many different Colours and Smell under his Feet to tread on; before and on each side of him, was fine lofty Trees of various Forms and Height, cloath'd with pleasant greed Leaves trim'd with rich Blossoms of many Colours to divert his Eye; a Number of several sorts of melodious Singing-Birds pearching in their most lovely Shades, as tho' Nature had studies to excel Man's brightest Imagination and Exquisiteness of Art". Peter Longueville, *The Hermit, or, the Unparalled Sufferings and Surprising Adventures of Mr Philip Quarll, an Englishman* (London: Printed by J. Cluer and A. Campbell, 1727), 247. However, throughout the novel these moments are consistently allegorised, so that the island maintains its religious dimension. The Rousseuvian trends that I am going to elaborate upon foreground a psychological or secularly spiritual, rather than religious, ideal of unity with nature.
16 August Fryderyk Moszyński, *Rozprawa o ogrodnictwie angielskim, 1774*, ed. Agnieszka Morawińska (Wrocław: Zakład Narodowy im. Ossolińskich, 1977), 110, trans. mine.
17 Mary L. Bellhouse, "On Understanding Rousseau's Praise of Robinson Crusoe", *Canadian Journal of Social and Political Theory/Revue canadienne de theorie politique et sociale* 6–3 (1982): 21.
18 Jean-Jacques Rousseau, "Julie, or the New Heloise", in *The Collected Writings of Rousseau*, vol. 6, trans. Philip Stewart and Jean Vache (Hanover, NH: University Press of New England, 1997), 387.
19 Jean-Jacques Rousseau, *The Reveries of a Solitary*, trans. John Gould Fletcher (New York: Burt Franklin, 1971), 110–111.
20 David Blewett, *The Illustration of Robinson Crusoe, 1719–1920* (Gerrards Cross: Smythe, 1995), 45–48.
21 David Blewett, "The Iconic Crusoe: Illustrations and Images of *Robinson Crusoe*", in *The Cambridge Companion to "Robinson Crusoe"*, ed. John Richetti (Cambridge: Cambridge University Press, 2018), 166.

22   Blewett, *The Illustration of* Robinson Crusoe, 49.
23   Blewett, "The Iconic Crusoe", 166.
24   Blewett, "The Iconic Crusoe", 166.
25   Robert Marzec, *An Ecological and Postcolonial Study of Literature: From Daniel Defoe to Salman Rushdie* (New York: Palgrave, 2007), 3.
26   Philip V. Allingham, "Thomas Stothard's *Robinson Crusoe and Friday making a tent to lodge Friday's father and the Spaniard*", 2018, Web. 3.02.2020. www.victorianweb.org/art/illustration/stothard/19.html.
27   William Hogarth, *The Analysis of Beauty*, ed. Ronald Paulson (New Haven and London: Yale University Press, 1997), 53.
28   Blewett, *The Illustration of* Robinson Crusoe, 52.
29   As Robert L. Patten puts it, Stothard "responded to developments in landscape gardening and the picturesque. Crusoe's island was a kind of paradise, and Crusoe's labours looked easy and successful". Robert L. Patten, *George Cruikshank's Life, Times, and Art. Volume 1: 1792–1835* (New Brunswick: Rutgers University Press, 1992), 336.
30   Simon Bainbridge (ed.), *Romanticism: A Sourcebook* (Houndmills: Palgrave Macmillan, 2008), 261.

2 Philip James de Loutherbourg's "Gothic" *Tom Jones*

In a well-known reading of Henry Fielding's *Tom Jones*, Dorothy van Ghent came up with the following architectural parallel: "We may think of *Tom Jones* as a complete architectural figure, a Palladian palace perhaps ... The structure is all but in the light of intelligibility: air circulates around and over it and through it".[1] The parallel proved attractive enough to be elaborated upon by others. Frederick Hilles offered a comparative reading of Fielding's novel and his friend Ralph Allen's Palladian mansion Prior Park on the outskirts of Bath, which was designed by John Wood the Younger, also the author of the celebrated Royal Crescent.[2] Martin Battestin, too, indicated that real life estates would have been the implied presence behind Fielding's narrative composition: "The same axioms that determined the form of Ralph Allen's 'stately house' at Prior Park or Lord Pembroke's bridge at Wilton have, in a sense, determined the form of *Tom Jones*".[3] As such, Fielding's novel used to be treated as sharp contrast to the emerging Gothic novel, characterised by loose organisation and occasional lack of coherence. Seen in this light, the label "Gothic Fielding" is an oxymoron.

On the other hand, in the recent decades there have appeared some revisionist readings of Fielding and the origins of Gothic fiction, which, surprisingly enough, have pointed to the possible Gothic undertones in Fielding's Palladian aesthetic. Fielding's last novel *Amelia* has been seen as potentially the most Gothic, a standpoint that was encouraged by Claude Rawson's seminal reading of the novel as testimony to the gradual "darkening" of Fielding's literary mood and the fragmentation of a sense of totality he used to offer in the earlier texts.[4] Accordingly, for Scott Robertson in *Amelia*'s atmosphere and vivid representation of prison spaces "one can detect an early trace of what was to become a favourite motif of the gothic novel".[5] Arguably, the strongest claim for "Gothic Fielding" has been put forward by John Allen Stevenson in the essay "*Tom Jones*, Jacobitism, and the rise of Gothic". Stevenson makes his

DOI: 10.4324/9781003153016-4

point in a provocative manner: "I would like to complicate ... genealogical speculations a bit by introducing into the discussion a name and a title
never mentioned ... or mentioned only for purposes of contrast. I mean
Henry Fielding and *Tom Jones*".[6] The critic then continues by suggesting
that in introducing anti-Jacobite elements, manifesting "an oddly gothic
flavour", the writer "developed a rhetoric that, at times, bears a notable
resemblance to the world of gothic novels";[7] in particular, the Gothic
aspects in *Tom Jones* are the motif of "the ghostly persistence of a dead
claim" and the paradigm of doubling.[8]

My aim in this chapter will be to address the question of "Gothic
Fielding" on the aesthetic rather than ideological level, in order to con-
front the text with Philip James de Loutherbourg's drawings of selected
scenes. In particular, I will attempt to address the question of selection:
why would de Loutherbourg ignore the actual Gothic content in the novel
and "Gothicise" scenes having little in common with the target aesthetic?

When *Tom Jones* was written, the Gothic revival had not yet fully
affected the realm of fiction. On the other hand, its early phase – the
architectural revival – was already at its peak. It is a telling coincidence that
the foremost achievement of Georgian Gothic – Horace Walpole's
restructuring of the Strawberry Hill estate – was initiated in 1749, the year
of *Tom Jones*'s publication. As a matter of fact, in spite of the popular critical concept of Fielding's Palladianism, the author himself was allegedly
much more enthusiastic about the modern medievalist trends. This would
have been reflected by the choice of the "*Gothick* Stile" for Mr Allworthy's
estate Paradise Hall – the moral and narrative centre of *Tom Jones*. Martin
Battestin, the same who treated Ralph Allen's Prior Park as the Palladian
presence behind the composition of *Tom Jones*, elsewhere speculated about
the origins of Paradise Hall. He pointed to Sharpham House in Glaston-
bury, where Fielding was born,[9] and his acquaintance with the architect
Sanderson Miller, a close friend of Fielding's patron and model for Mr
Allworthy, George Lyttelton, for whom Miller designed Gothic embellishments, such as a miniature ruined castle, and was to have built a Gothic
house.[10] The house did not materialise in real life (due to Lyttelton's wife's
protests), but emerged as a literary one instead – in Mr Allworthy's Paradise Hall. The description of the estate is perhaps the most pictorial
moment in the entire narrative and deserves to be quoted in full:

> The Gothick Stile of Building could produce nothing nobler than
> Mr. *Allworthy's* House. There was an Air of Grandeur in it, that
> struck you with Awe, and rival'd the Beauties of the best Grecian
> Architecture; and it was as commodious within, as venerable
> without.

It stood on the South-east side of a Hill, but nearer the Bottom than the Top of it, so as to be sheltered from the North-east by a Grove of old Oaks, which rose above it in a gradual Ascent of near half a Mile, and yet high enough to enjoy a most charming Prospect of the Valley beneath.

In the midst of the Grove was a fine Lawn sloping down towards the House, near the Summit of which rose a plentiful Spring, gushing out of a Rock covered with Firs, and forming a constant Cascade of about thirty Foot, not carried down a regular Flight of Steps, but tumbling in a natural Fall over the broken and mossy Stones, till it came to the bottom of the Rock; then running off in a pebly Channel, that with many lesser Falls winded along, till it fell into a Lake at the Foot of the Hill, about a quarter of a Mile below the House on the South Side, and which was seen from every Room in the Front. Out of this Lake, which filled the Center of a beautiful Plain, embellished with Groupes of Beeches and Elms, and fed with Sheep, issued a River, that for several Miles was seen to meander through an amazing Variety of Meadows and Woods, till it emptied itself into the Sea, with a large Arm of which, and an Island beyond it, the Prospect was closed.

On the right of this Valley opened another of less Extent, adorned with several Villages, and terminated by one of the Towers of an old ruined Abbey, grown over with Ivy, and Part of the Front which remained still entire.

The left Hand Scene presented the View of a very fine Park, composed of very unequal Ground, and agreeably varied with all the Diversity that Hills, Lawns, Wood and Water, laid out with admirable Taste, but owing less to Art than to Nature, could give. Beyond this the country gradually rose into a Ridge of wild Mountains, the Tops of which were above the Clouds.[11]

Of course, this is not how Gothic castles would be described in late eighteenth-century fiction, but the passage does reveal some stock Gothic tropes that would later define the sentimental Gothic aesthetic in the 1780s and 1790s. In particular, it offers a reconciliation of what later aesthetic thinkers would distinguish as the sublime, the beautiful and the picturesque – a quality that was to become Ann Radcliffe's trademark several decades later. There is little that we know about the Gothic interiors of the estate, and Paradise Hall, ideologically speaking, does not become a space of entrapment and desubjectification[12] (even if it does become a setting for unjust persecution). On the other hand, the outsides, as depicted in the passage, as well as the precisely described environs, capture the essence of the mid-century architectural revival and also its artistic (visual and literary) representations: "an Air of Grandeur" striking with "Awe"; surrounding "mossy Stones" and rocks; the neighbourhood of "an old Ruined Abbey, grown over with Ivy"; and the background of "a Ridge of wild Mountains, the Tops of which were above the Clouds".

Paradise Hall was not the only Gothic edifice to embellish the pages of Fielding's fiction. *A Journey from this World to the Next* (1743), recounting the narrator's travels in the nether world, features the "palace of Death", the institutional centre of the underworld:

> Its outside, indeed, appeared extremely magnificent. Its structure was of the Gothic order; vast beyond imagination, the whole pile consisting of black marble. Rows of immense yews form an amphitheatre round it of such height and thickness that no ray of the sun ever perforates this grove, where black eternal darkness would reign was it not excluded by innumerable lamps which are placed in pyramids round the grove; so that the distant reflection they cast on the palace, which is plentifully gilt with gold on the outside, is inconceivably solemn. To this I may add the hollow murmur of winds constantly heard from the grove, and the very remote sound of roaring waters. Indeed, every circumstance seems to conspire to fill the mind with horrour and consternation as we approach to this palace.[13]

Despite the tinge of oriental fashions, the passage is reminiscent of contemporaneous descriptions of the prisons of the Inquisition, an analogy that seems supported by the traveller's encounter with "an inquisitor-general" inside. Similar edifices can be found in imprisonment narratives, which, in turn, had an impact on late eighteenth-century Gothic fiction. For example, in Ann Radcliffe's *The Italian* (1796–1797) the prisons of the Inquisition are made of "walls, of immense height, and strengthened by innumerable massy bulwarks" and look like "a vast and dreary blank".[14] This time Fielding does present the interiors of the place, but again, they do not match the atmosphere of Gothic dread produced by the outside: "this palace, so awful and tremendous without, is all gay and sprightly within; ... we soon lost all those dismal and gloomy ideas we had contracted in approaching it".[15]

In *Tom Jones*, then, Fielding not only repeated the idea to make a Gothic mansion the centre of the universe, but also followed the very same agenda of a discrepancy between the outside and the inside. "Horrour" and "Awe" inspired by the Gothic are counterbalanced by the comforting interiors. In this, Fielding's Gothic moments are illustrative of eighteenth-century medievalism before the emergence of Gothic fiction, when quasi-medieval architectural elements typically enriched homely spaces. The literary transformation of the Gothic setting into a space of danger can be traced in Horace Walpole's transposition of Strawberry Hill into the realm of fiction. In a well-known letter to his friend William Cole (9 March 1765), Walpole identified the origins of *The Castle of Otranto* (1764) in a nightmare that he had in his Gothic villa, as well as drawing parallels between his house and the fictitious castle.[16] The discrepancy between the brightly coloured and lavish Strawberry Hill estate and the Gothic castle in the novel is striking, and this would have been noticed by the illustrators of *The Castle of Otranto*. As Peter Lindfield has shown, the subsequent illustrators of *Otranto* did not follow up on Walpole's suggestion to perceive the castle through the prism of Strawberry Hill and depicted the setting as properly Gothic and properly medieval.[17]

I would now like to bridge the gap between *Tom Jones* and de Loutherbourg's drawings by recapitulating on what I have written so far. Architectural medievalism in the 1740s and 1750s laid the foundations of the literary Gothic revival on the aesthetic level by introducing pictorial motifs that would prove highly inspirational in the period of the "efflorescence" of the Gothic. On the other hand, as represented by Fielding, the mid-century Gothic depended on an aesthetic of "simulacrum", as Jean Baudrillard would have it.[18] That is, it did not produce any Gothic essence and depended on the policy of "void" imitation. As Jerrold Hogle has written on Strawberry Hill, it was generally fake; something depending for its identity on imitation and multiplication of Gothic elements as known from prints, catalogues and other visual sources – an edifice without an essential, architectural identity.[19] Fielding's mansions illustrate this inner emptiness – they are Gothic only on the outside.

It is now 1775 and a popular painter of sublime and picturesque sceneries, including Gothic ruins and castles, turns to *Tom Jones*. In 1775, the Swiss-French artist Philip James de Loutherbourg (1740–1812) had lived in London for only four years and was still in the process of making his name. His biggest achievements were to come in 1781, when he became a member of the Royal Academy and started putting on his quasi-theatricals known as the *Eidophusikon*. In the meantime, de Loutherbourg was employed by David Garrick at the Drury Lane Theatre to work on scenery, costumes and the machinery and was exhibiting the kind of paintings he had been known for to the Parisian audiences, including "landscapes, pastorals, *banditti*, and shipwrecks".[20]

The *Tom Jones* drawings, given the size and format, would have been meant for display beyond the book context – not as illustrations but as framed exhibits. The first was *Tom Jones, assisting Molly Seagrim, In the Church Yard and Repelling her Adversaries* drawn in 1775 (Figure 2.1) and engraved shortly after by the popular engraver Joseph Bartalozzi. The second piece was *A Boxing Match*, now lost, which de Loutherbourg exhibited at the Royal Academy in 1776. Later, it was engraved by Victor Marie Picot as *Tom Jones & Mr Western Combating with Blifil and Thwackum* (Figure 2.2). There was certainly a third roundel, also lost – *Tom Jones Threatening Partridge* – preserved in an engraving by Picot (Figure 2.3). There might have been other drawings, too: a 1780 *Catalogue of Prints* lists "Four circles" from *Tom Jones* after de Loutherbourg,[21] whereas the estate sale on 19 June 1812 listed 11 prints from *Tom Jones*. [22] There is no way of proving, though, that these prints were not repeated, that initially there were 11 original drawings.

Figure 2.1 Philip James de Loutherbourg, "Tom Jones Assisting Molly Sea-grim in the Churchyard", 1775. The Metropolitan Museum of Art. Gift of Joseph Baillio, in honour of Philippe de Montebello, 2008.

Figure 2.2 Victor Marie Picot, after Philip James de Loutherbourg, "Tom Jones & Mr Western Combating with Blifil and Thwackum", 1782. Yale University Art Gallery.

The drawings are good illustrations of the artist's manner – a successful blend of French rococo and Salvator Rosa-like sublime and picturesque qualities. When in England, de Loutherbourg was true to his original aesthetic, as well as welcoming the particularities of the English landscape, including products of the Gothic revival, still at its peak in the final decades of the eighteenth century.

Figure 2.3 Victor Marie Picot, after Philip James de Loutherbourg, "Tom
Jones Threatening Patridge", 1782. Yale University Art Gallery.

What certainly draws attention is de Loutherbourg's selection of material. The painter does not choose the originally Gothic content, the possible
reason for which I have addressed before. Nor does he represent the scenes
that are the most important for the narrative or the most iconic. The choice
of the mock-heroic battle in the churchyard cannot surprise; even if it is
only a peripheral embellishment in Fielding's novel, it is a truly memorable
one. The other two scenes, in turn, depict moments that even a careful

reader of *Tom Jones* would find difficult to locate immediately. Be that as it may, the three pictures are very much similar, and the similarities are both structural and thematic. First of all, in a manner reminiscent of Salvator Rosa, de Loutherbourg stages figures of rather limited size against domineering backgrounds. In the first drawing, Tom Jones defends Molly in the shadow of an impressive parish church, the size of which would have been much more appropriate for a cathedral or an abbey. The Gothic church is conveniently grown over with ivy and partially covered by the ominous tree branch. In the second print, Tom Jones and Partridge are dwarfed by an old tree reminiscent of the one in the previous picture, and the scene is set against a natural background, revealing the top of a Gothic tower in the centre. In the third print, the figures are again dominated by natural scenery complemented by the monument on the right, this time reminiscent of the French rococo. As for the thematic choices, the three pictures depict characters engaged in fights, from the mock-heroic battle in a church cemetery, which, however, is here deprived of the mocking dimension, to vivid fisticuffs.

As I mentioned before, de Loutherbourg's drawings are not strictly speaking illustrations; nevertheless, I do think it is possible to approach them as such. Writing about book illustration in the eighteenth century, Philip Stewart points out that even if the text does not determine the way it is illustrated, "there are ways in which it can flag the attention of a potential illustrator".[23] On the other hand, it is possible for the illustrator to engage with the text by way of exposing, and thus emphasising, scenes that are not necessarily central to the narrative. If this be the case, playing the role of a framing device, illustrations may suggest alternative readings and negotiate the alleged "authorial message". De Loutherbourg's pieces exemplify the second possibility – they do not seem to depict what might have been possibly "flagged" by Fielding; on the contrary, they frame *Tom Jones* as the kind of story it is not, with a quasi-Gothic or Salvator Rosa-like universe of gloomy natural settings and *banditti* (see Figure 2.4). De Loutherbourg picked those scenes that allowed for their transposition into the genre of "landscape with bandits", thus adapting the narrative to the pre-Romantic tastes of the 1770s and 1780s. Salvatorian landscapes with *banditti* enjoyed a considerable popularity in the 1770s, also in the circles of the Royal Academy. Apart from de Loutherbourg, the other important painter who exhibited *banditti* at the time was John Hamilton Mortimer (1740–1779), whose "manner" proved attractive for a number of imitators.

Coming to a conclusion, I would argue that de Loutherbourg's strategies of de-contextualisation and re-contextualisation should be seen in the light of the fashion for anthologies known as *"The Beauties of..."*. The first *Beauties of Fielding* were published in 1782 (followed by two further

Figure 2.4 Salvator Rosa, "Bandits on a Rocky Coast", 1655–1660. The Metropolitan Museum of Art. Charles B. Curtis Fund, 1934.

editions in the same year; it might not have been a coincidence that the two prints were also engraved in 1782), but they were preceded by a number of multi-author anthologies, such as *The Beauties of English Prose* (1772). The drawings stem from the same agenda of depriving the selected scenes and passages of their original contexts and adjusting them to the target aesthetic. When *Tom Jones* was first published, many of its critical readers pointed to immoral content. But only a few decades later, the 1782 anthology adjusted Fielding's aesthetic to the prevalent sentimental tastes. The backmatter blurb of *The Beauties of Fielding* promotes the series as a way to "inform the understanding, and entertain the imagination",[24] but this was meant to be achieved by substantial editorial interference. S.T. Coleridge would later consider these anthologies as "injurious to the original Author" and "disorganizing his productions".[25] Indeed, aligning Fielding's work to the anthologist's policy came at a cost: as Daniel Cook puts it, "No brothels, adultery, nakedness, bawdy language, or even Tom Jones's many escapades, are to be found in *The Beauties of Fielding*".[26] If "sentimental Fielding" was a possibility, then "Gothic Fielding" was another one.

Figure 2.5 Francesco Bartolozzi, after Philip James de Loutherbourg. "The Snuff Box – Calais", 1799. The British Museum. © Trustees of the British Museum.

The most popular author in *The Beauties of...* series was Laurence Sterne. Here, homogenising the author meant side-lining the Shandean ambiguities and constructing "a fully sanitized, alphabetized handbook of Sterne's sentiments on such topics as beauty, charity, and forgiveness".[27] When de Loutherbourg turned to Sterne in 1799, his choices were everything but surprising. The scenes he illustrated, "The Snuff Box – Calais" (Figure 2.5) and the "Dead Ass – Nampont", constitute the core of *A Sentimental Journey*'s panorama of sensibility.

The elements of Salvatorian iconography that these two pictures preserve, such as the waving tree branches, elaborative foliage and overgrown architectural elements, do not in any way compromise the sentimentalism of the scenes. The case of de Loutherbourg's Sterne, then, is different, in as much as the patterns of homogenisation, the toning down of ambiguities, differ from transvaluation. It is, of course, paradoxical that in adapting *Tom Jones* for the Gothic tastes de Loutherbourg ignores the actual Gothic content. But this choice, in a way, is illustrative of the discontinuities in the Gothic tradition itself; in other words, the divide separating the aesthetic of the architectural Gothic revival and late eighteenth-century Gothic fiction. There may be traces of the former in Fielding's narrative, but in the three pictures I have shown de Loutherbourg draws the novel closer to the latter tradition.

Notes

This chapter is an updated and developed version of the following article: Jakub Lipski, "Gothic Fielding? Philip James de Loutherbourg's *Tom Jones*", *Porównania* 21 (2017): 259–267.

1　Dorothy van Ghent, *The English Novel: Form and Function* (New York: Rhinehart, 1953), 80.
2　Frederick Hilles, "Art and Artifice in *Tom Jones*", in *Imagined Worlds: Essays on Some English Novels and Novelists in Honour of John Butt*, ed. Maynard Mack and Ian Gregor (London: Methuen, 1968), 91–110.
3　Martin C. Battestin, *The Providence of Wit: Aspects of Form in Augustan Literature and the Arts* (Oxford: Clarendon Press, 1974), 149.
4　Claude Julien Rawson, *Henry Fielding and the Augustan Ideal under Stress: "Nature's Dances of Death" and Other Studies* (London and Boston: Routledge and Kegan Paul, 1972), 96–97.
5　Scott Robertson, *Henry Fielding: Literary and Theological Misplacement* (Bern: Peter Lang, 2010), 176.
6　John Allen Stevenson, "*Tom Jones*, Jacobitism, and the Rise of Gothic", in *Gothic Origins and Innovations*, ed. Allan Lloyd Smith and Victor Sage (Amsterdam and Atlanta: Rodopi, 1994), 16.
7　Stevenson, "*Tom Jones*, Jacobitism, and the Rise of Gothic", 16.
8　Stevenson, "*Tom Jones*, Jacobitism, and the Rise of Gothic", 21.
9　Martin C. Battestin, *A Henry Fielding Companion* (Westport and London: Greenwood Press, 2000), 1.
10　Battestin, *A Henry Fielding Companion*, 101.
11　Henry Fielding, *The History of Tom Jones, A Foundling*, ed. Martin C. Battestin and Fredson Bowers (Middletown: Wesleyan University Press, 1975), 42–43.
12　David Punter and Glennis Byron, *The Gothic* (Oxford: Blackwell, 2004), 261–262.
13　Henry Fielding, *A Journey from this World to the Next*, ed. Claude Rawson (London: Dent, 1973), 20–21.
14　Ann Radcliffe, *The Italian*, ed. E.J. Clery (Oxford: Oxford University Press, 2008), 196.

15 Fielding, *A Journey from this World to the Next*, 21.
16 Horace Walpole, *The Yale Edition of Horace Walpole's Correspondence*, ed. W.S. Lewis et al. (New Haven and London: Yale University Press, 1937–1983), vol.1, 88.
17 Peter N. Lindfield, "Imagining the Undefined Castle in *The Castle of Otranto*: Engravings and Interpretations", *Image [&] Narrative* 18.3 (2017): 46–63.
18 See Jean Baudrillard, *Simulacra and Simulation*, trans. Sheila Faria Glaser (1981; Ann Arbor: University of Michigan Press, 2008).
19 Jerrold E. Hogle, "The Ghost of the Counterfeit in the Genesis of the Gothic", in *Gothic Origins and Innovations*, ed. Allan Lloyd Smith and Victor Sage (Amsterdam and Atlanta: Rodopi, 1994), 23.
20 Gloria Groom, "Art, Illustration, and Enterprise in Late Eighteenth-Century English Art: A Painting by Philippe Jacques de Loutherbourg", *Art Institute of Chicago Museum Studies* 18.2 (1992): 127.
21 *A Catalogue of Prints and Books of Prints* (London: Hooper and Davis, 1780), 40.
22 See Perrin Stein and Mary Tavener Holmes, *Eighteenth-Century French Drawings in New York Collections* (New York: The Metropolitan Museum of Art, 1999), 164.
23 Philip Stewart, *Engraven Desire: Eros, Image & Text in the French Eighteenth Century* (Durham and London: Duke University Press, 1992), 2.
24 *The Beauties of Fielding: Carefully Selected from the Works of that Eminent Writer. To which is added Some Account of his Life* (London: G. Kearsley, 1782).
25 Samuel Taylor Coleridge, Letter to John Murray (18 January 1822), in *Collected Letters of Samuel Taylor Coleridge*, ed. Earl Leslie Griggs, vol. 5 (Oxford: Clarendon Press, 1971), 200. See M-C. Newbould, "Wit and Humour for the Heart of Sensibility: The Beauties of Fielding and Sterne", in *The Afterlives of Eighteenth-Century Fiction*, ed. Daniel Cook and Nicholas Seager (Cambridge: Cambridge University Press, 2015), 133.
26 Daniel Cook, "Authors Unformed: Reading 'Beauties' in the Eighteenth Century", *Philological Quarterly* 89.2–3 (2010): 290.
27 Cook, "Authors Unformed", 290.

Part II
Reception in Poland

3   The Early Reception of *Robinson Crusoe* in Poland

The Adventures of Mr. Nicholas Wisdom by Ignacy Krasicki (1776) is a typical starting point for historical investigations into the development of the modern novel in Polish literature.[1] For one thing, it is difficult not to admit the novelty of the narrative in the context of the romance tradition dominating the realm of prose narrative in the preceding decades: Krasicki's book has been labelled "anti-romance" to highlight the difference on the grounds of its openly parodic undertones.[2] For another thing, the figure of the author, which in Polish literature is comparable to that of Alexander Pope,[3] legitimates attempts to put him in the role of originator or trend setter. Indeed, the critics of the Enlightenment in Poland, especially the Stanislavian Age – the reign of King Stanislaus (1764–1795), who ushered in far-reaching cultural reforms – have been basically unanimous in labelling the narrative "the first Polish novel".[4]

Derivative as it was, *Nicholas Wisdom* transposed onto Polish soil a number of narrative conventions that had already been flourishing in French and English literature (the two main points of reference for Krasicki and the other Stanislavian *literati*). A first-person narrative, the novel opens in a manner typical of fictional memoirs. Nicholas is a member of the Polish nobility and is about to learn what the world is like. The first section recounts his childhood, education and Grand Tour, recycling elements known from didactic rake's progresses in the Hogarthian style, such as gambling and amorous misfortunes. It closes with the Robinsonade moment, when Nicholas is marooned on an unknown island. This is followed by the utopian section featuring the happy Nipuans living in a state of nature. In this part, Nicholas receives his "natural" education from Master Xaoo and changes his worldview. In the third section, Nicholas returns to Europe and Poland and has a chance to understand the superiority of the Nipuan ideas over the civilised customs and political relations on the Continent and in his own motherland.

DOI: 10.4324/9781003153016-6

Toward the end of the utopian section (Chapter 15, Book 2), shortly before Nicholas is able to leave the island on a boat he has himself mended and prepared for departure, the protagonist enters the wreck of the ship that marooned him. Like Robinson, Nicholas retrieves a number of goods, which he then stores in a cave. He then presents a meticulous list of items retrieved, in a manner imitating Crusoe's systematic discourse. This is perhaps the closest Krasicki gets to the Defoevian idiom, but such moments do not dominate the narrative. In total, the motifs that Krasicki would have taken from *Robinson Crusoe* include storm and shipwreck, initial despair on the beach and fear of wilderness, re-entering the wreck, using a cave as a store, rescue from a Spanish ship and imprisonment by a slave trader sailing to Brazil. In addition, the narrative occasionally echoes Robinson's reflective passages, concerned with the role of Providence and self-analysis, such as the following: "Walking alone along the coast line, exactly where I had been cast away, I started reflecting upon my present condition and, in general, upon all of my life's adventures".[5] As indicated above, *Nicholas Wisdom* can be considered not a fully-fledged Robinsonade but a quasi-Robinsonade at best, not least because of the fact that the crucial shipwreck and island motif is promptly transformed into a utopian narrative,[6] which, in turn, does not take more than a third of the whole novel. Admittedly, the reader of *Nicholas Wisdom* is bound to recognise that Krasicki would have been equally indebted to Jonathan Swift and his *Gulliver's Travels* (1726), and perhaps more to Jean-Jacques Rousseau's *Emile* (1762) and Voltaire's *Candide* (1759).[7] Nevertheless, the diffused elements of Wisdom's Robinsonade, even if indirectly, begin a relatively rich tradition of Polish reworkings of the pattern,[8] which, however, would not develop properly until the nineteenth century. The best-known and most successful Robinsonades in Polish include works by Władysław Ludwik Anczyc (1823–1883), who also abbreviated *Robinson Crusoe* in 1867, Adolf Dygasiński (1839–1902) and Arkady Fiedler (1894–1985), the author of the Robinson trilogy including *Wyspa Robinsona* (Robinson Crusoe Island, 1954), *Orinoko* (Orinoco, 1957) and *Biały Jaguar* (White Jaguar, 1980). Implicit uses and references to the Robinsonade topoi and iconography can also be recognised in the work of Julian Ursyn Niemcewicz (1758–1841)[9] and – most famously, perhaps – in Nobel Laureate Henryk Sienkiewicz's *In Desert and Wilderness* (1911).

Back in the late eighteenth century, Robinsonade motifs were immediately re-adopted by Krasicki in his *History* (1779) – a novel inspired by the tradition of imaginary voyages and dialogues with the dead. In *History*, the time-travelling narrator is at one point tired of the world and decides to retire into the wild. He finds a pleasant mountainous spot somewhere in China and is bent on spending his days "in peace" and "far from human company".[10] Like Robinson, Krasicki's time traveller re-enacts the story of agricultural and civilisational change:

> When I had enough wood at my disposal, I built myself a hut – a dwelling not magnificent but comfortable. I started to work the land: I planted seeds of vegetables and herbs that appeared edible and ended up being very well provided ... . Then I caught a few deer-like animals, still rather little. I tamed them so well that they would not leave me for a second. I did the same with various species of bird. They would sing songs to me and I fed them as the land was fertile.
>
> Necessity is the mother of invention, so I learnt to be proficient in all the crafts.[11]

Although he published *History* three years after *Nicholas Wisdom*, Krasicki was in fact working on the two texts almost at the same time,[12] which may lead to the conclusion that despite the brevity of the two Robinsonade sections, the novelist was elaborating on a convention and an idea that were thought topical and relevant at the time of writing. The specificity of the historical moment is all the more significant as the Robinsonade proper, as a fully-fledged genre, did not start to develop in Polish literature before the mid-nineteenth century. This chapter locates Krasicki's interest in the Robinsonade in the literary and intellectual context of the author's time, in particular in the several years preceding the writing and publication of *Nicholas Wisdom*, beginning with the 1760s – a decade of changes in the literary tastes ushered in by the Anglophile King Stanislaus August Poniatowski – and then moving on to the 1770s and beyond. The first Polish translation of *Robinson Crusoe* in 1769 will be seen as a response to the heightened interest in Defoe's novel in the 1760s, while the subsequent editions in the 1770s and finally the publication of *Nicholas Wisdom* in 1776 will be taken as testimony to the enduring presence of *Crusoe* in the literary life of the Stanislavian Age, in a decade characterised by a growing demand for prose fiction.

Tellingly enough, the 1769 translation was the first translation of an English novel into Polish, with the others not coming before the late 1770s. In the same year, the flourishing demand for narratives of adventures and sentimental affairs was satiated by Polish translations of Alain-René Le Sage's *Gil Blas* (1715–1735) and Antoine Prévost's *Manon Lescaut* (1731). As Jan van der Meer points out, in 1769 the number of modern novels published in Poland for the first time exceeded ten.[13] Van der Meer later indicates that the real change in the novel production was brought in 1776, when *Nicholas Wisdom* was published.[14] The period studied here, then, framed by these two publishing events, appears to have been the formative time for the development of the modern novel in Polish. In reconstructing this historical moment, I show how the publication of the first Polish translation of Defoe's novel testified to some of the strategies characterising the literary life of Warsaw at the beginning of King Stanislaus's reign. The appearance of *Robinson Crusoe* and the Robinsonade in Poland was a multifaceted literary event, which involved the king's close circle of literary associates and some of the most influential figures in the literary sphere.

The early reception of *Robinson Crusoe* on Polish soil exemplifies the general tendencies in the afterlife of English fiction in Enlightenment Poland. First of all, the translations came out relatively late, just as the market for modern prose narrative started to develop several decades later than in England and France, basically with King Stanislaus's succession to the throne and the proper beginning of the Polish Enlightenment (the preceding reign of August III is usually considered as the final stage of the Baroque). Second, a number of English novels were translated not from the original but from the French versions, often rather loose and abbreviated. Finally, *Robinson Crusoe's* early reception in Poland, just like the reception of the other highlights of modern fiction (for example, Le Sage, Henry Fielding and Laurence Sterne) is to be credited to the circle of King Stanislaus – a trendsetter in modern Enlightenment culture and the early stages of Polish Anglophilia. The Stanislavian period was the time when the love for things French in Poland was gradually accompanied by the love for things English (often through French mediation). There have appeared studies of the phenomenon in Polish criticism, but the emphasis has been placed on such "isms" as sternism, discussed in this book too, and ossianism.[15]

Richard Butterwick suggests that translations of English novels were conducted independently of the king and that the king's Anglophilia "remained largely a private matter".[16] This might have been the case when one searches for explicit commissions and archival remnants of influence. However, I argue that literary phenomena should not be analysed in this manner only. The Royal Library in Warsaw was far from being a private sphere and exerted an impact on the women and men of letters, including Ignacy Krasicki,[17] who gathered their own collections and modelled them on the one owned by the monarch. The king's circle of friends were affected by his tastes, as revealed in the rich literary life of the Czartoryski circle, first in Warsaw and then in Puławy (see Chapter 4). I do not claim that the king alone was instrumental in the early reception of *Robinson Crusoe* in Poland; rather, the literary life of the Royal Castle was an important, if not the most important, element in the intellectual network of the 1760s and 1770s, which was the scene for the appearance of Defoe's novel in Poland.

Though fiction did not dominate the collection, the king and his librarians were responsive to the modern trends in narrative prose. *Robinson Crusoe* was one of the first novels to be ordered for the library. An early receipt for books obtained in the period between 1767 and 1775, the first extensive list of books for the royal library, features a three-volume French edition ("*La vie et avantures de Robinson Crusoe*, t. 1–3, Paris 1761") and a two-volume English edition. The list includes 278 titles, so no hasty conclusions should be drawn from the presence of Defoe's novel. However, bearing in mind the fact that the market for prose narrative was to start developing at the turn of the 1760s and 1770s, the few novels included should be taken seriously. The canonical examples of modern prose fiction first ordered by the king and his librarians included only the following: Le Sage's *Gil Blas* in the first Polish translation from 1769; Marie Jeanne Riccoboni's *Lettres de Milady Juliette Catesby* (1760) in the original, which was promoted by Voltaire himself; and Sterne's *A Sentimental Journey* (1768) in the French translation by Frenais; the rest was dominated by travels, histories and philosophical treatises. It should be noted that only *Robinson Crusoe* was included in two different editions, including an English edition.[18] By the 1760s, King Stanislaus had acquired the necessary command of the English language, as testified by his correspondence with English diplomat Sir Charles H. Williams, who was instrumental in the evolution of Stanislaus's taste for England and English culture.[19] *Crusoe* was also collected in the other significant libraries of the nobility in the Stanislavian period (including Ignacy Krasicki's library): Zofia Sinko located 11 copies throughout the country, which is one of the highest numbers for novels translated into Polish in the 1760s and 1770s.[20] Needless to say, library collections should not be treated as decisive evidence for anything other than themselves, but it is worth bearing them in mind when reconstructing the literary scene.

The receipt also provides insight into the prospective ways modern fiction in Polish was to start developing, the dominant points of reference being the picaresque and the sentimental. Admittedly, *Robinson Crusoe* in the 1760s was read as belonging and contributing to both variants, given the adventurous element, on the one hand, and the commentary on a state of nature, on the other. Generically heterogeneous as it was, Krasicki's *Nicholas Wisdom* encapsulated these conventions, beginning like a rake's progress tinged with sentimental affairs (Nicholas repeatedly refers to his "sentimental education"), only to become a Rousseauvian utopia in Book II.

One does not risk much interpreting the early reception of *Robinson Crusoe* in Poland in the context of Jean-Jacques Rousseau's thought. The interest in Defoe's novel among the Polish intellectual elite was most likely due to the famous recommendation put forward by Rousseau in his *Emile, or On Education* (1762). *Emile* was known and read in Poland, though not uncritically, already in the 1760s,[21] and the periodical *Monitor*, modelled on the *Spectator*, published excerpts from the treatise in 1765 (nos. 31–32). The utopian section of Krasicki's *Nicholas Wisdom* promotes a system of education very much in line with the ideas of the French philosopher: the teacher first learns about the pupil and then tries to eliminate the wrong habits so as to be certain that the seeds of moral truths he proceeds to plant will fall upon clean and fertile soil; finally, he ensures that the theory will be successfully put in practice.[22] Having been taught the Nipuan way of life and gradually coming to realise the artificiality of "civilised" societies, Nicholas has no alternative but to accept the superiority of the Nipuans. He now understands why he himself is being called a "savage", thus self-reflexively implying that in Krasicki's Robinsonade the role of Friday is reserved for the marooned protagonist.

Rousseau's thought fuelled the French reception of Defoe's novel, with a visible increase in the number of editions published.[23] In 1766 a new translation/adaptation by Joseph Feutry (1720–1789) appeared,[24] which would serve as the model for the translator into Polish. As for the recommendation itself, *Crusoe* is promoted as "the most felicitous treatise on natural education":

> This book will be the first that my Emile will read. For a long time it will alone compose his whole library, and it will always hold a distinguished place there. It will be the text for which all our discussions on the natural sciences will serve only as commentary. It will serve as a test of the condition of our judgment during our progress, and so long as our taste is not spoiled, its reading will always please us.[25]

The remark is then followed by Rousseau's interpretation of the model including a clearer formulation of its educational merits:

> Robinson Crusoe on his island, alone, deprived of the assistance of his kind and the instruments of all the arts, providing nevertheless for his subsistence, for his preservation, and even procuring for himself a kind of well-being – this is an object interesting for every age and one which can be made agreeable to children in countless ways ... The surest means of raising oneself above prejudices and

ordering one's judgments about the true relations of things is to put oneself in the place of an isolated man and to judge everything as this man himself ought to judge with respect to his own utility.
...

This novel, disencumbered of all its rigmarole, beginning with Robinson's shipwreck near the island and ending with the arrival of the ship which comes to take him from it, will be both Emile's entertainment and instruction throughout the period which is dealt with here.[26]

Rousseau's interpretation, in a way, gave way to some dominant reception trends in the later decades of the eighteenth century, irrespective of what the novel was really like. These, at least to some extent, were based on misconceptions. First, Crusoe was not deprived of "instruments of all the arts", and rather than establishing himself on the island from scratch, he depends on the remnants of civilisation that he has managed to retrieve from the ship. Second, Rousseau's remark that the book can be "made agreeable to children in countless ways" implied the potential of the story to become children's literature – a quality that would not have been projected by Defoe.[27] Finally, the French thinker appears to have appreciated only the island section of the narrative, which in Defoe's novel is only part of a larger, much more complex whole. The rest is dubbed "rigmarole" and considered redundant. These three observations formed a model of reception that, arguably, survived in the popular imagination well into the twenty-first century. More immediately, in turn, it provided a formula for what might be termed the Rousseauvian Robinsonade, "beginning with Robinson's shipwreck near the island and ending with the arrival of the ship which comes to take him from it", suited particularly for adolescent readers. The first of this kind was Joachim Heinrich Campe's *Robinson der Jüngere* from 1779, which immediately became very popular reading throughout Europe. The Polish translation (1793) was promoted in a way that foregrounded the still prevalent Rousseauvian understanding of *Crusoe* as implied in the publishing announcement of the new version: "This work ... is one of the best to shape a child's heart and mind. It teaches in an entertaining manner and does not cause the young reader's interest to wane".[28] It is worth recalling that the reception of *Crusoe* in Rousseau's manner transcended the confines of literature and entered garden design, as discussed in Chapter 1 with reference to August Fryderyk Moszyński's idea for "Robinson Crusoe's habitation" in his *Essay sur le jardinage Anglois*.

Having sketched the background for the appearance of *Robinson Crusoe* in Poland, it is now time to introduce the two main agents of this literary event – the translator and the publisher. Jan Chrzciciel (Giovanni Battista) Albertrandi, the first translator of *Robinson Crusoe*, was closely affiliated with the king: first as his reader, then librarian and finally principal archivist. Like the king himself, Albertrandi cooperated with Michał Gröll – a German printer who moved to Warsaw from Dresden and established a printing house that would dominate the literary scene of the late 1760s and 1770s. Following the modus operandi adopted in Western Europe, Gröll published not only popular works of fiction but also literary periodicals that set the ground for the books by way of reviews, publishing announcements and essays aimed at shaping the literary taste. The best-known fruit of Albertrandi and Gröll's cooperation was the literary weekly *Zabawy przyjemne i pożyteczne* (Pleasant and Useful Diversions, 1770–1777), which energised the literary life of Warsaw in accord with the ideas of the king (duly supported in the weekly). It was published by Gröll and edited by Albertrandi.

As for the 1769 translation itself,[29] the paratext of the edition consists of several aspects that should be noted here. The book opens with a dedication to Lady Jadwiga Lubieńska, who is credited with having provided the translator with the time and space needed for the carrying out of the translation: the work began in 1767 and took Albertrandi six weeks. Then comes the translator's preface, which is an important contribution to the developing novelistic discourse in Poland. The periodical *Monitor* was known for its criticism of romance writing, thus setting the scene for the emergence of realist fiction. Albertrandi in his preface anticipates the possible criticism for presenting the Polish readers with "another Romance" and recycles the common remarks used to denigrate the genre: irrationality, no applicability to real life and waste of readers' time (vii–viii). Then, the translator proceeds to argue for *Robinson Crusoe*'s distinctiveness from the romance tradition, referring to the examples of Fénelon and Ramsey (the translator of Fénelon and author of the popular *Travels of Cyrus* from 1727, Polish translation in 1770): "In contrast to their works, what we learn from the adventures of Robinson is applicable in everyday life" (ix). Robinson is understood to exemplify the instability of the human mind, the workings of Providence, courage, hard work and prudence. All these, the translator has it, are to be taught to people, and the attractive form of history makes it easier and more delightful (x). The conclusion accords with the *utile et dulce* principle – it is not a waste of time if entertainment becomes a form of education.

The apologetic passage is then complemented by the so-called "uwiadomienie" – a short note about the book, its author and publication context. It contains a factual error, which, however, may tell us more about the Polish context for the appearance of *Robinson Crusoe*. The writer credited with authoring *Robinson Crusoe* is Richard Steele, who is praised as the principal contributor to the *Spectator*, a periodical published to "correct the habits and customs" of people and repeatedly referred to and translated in "our Monitor" (xi). Intentionally or not, by linking the release of his translation of *Robinson Crusoe* with the intellectual policy of the *Monitor*, Albertrandi not only highlights its difference from the romance tradition but also argues for its applicability to the intellectual programme of the Warsaw literary and political elite. Apparently, the Polish translator is repeating the error made by Feutry, who misattributed the novel to Steele in his own preface to the 1766 French translation. The likely reason for the confusion was Steele's role in popularising the history of Alexander Selkirk, which, however, used the platform of another journal – the *Englishman* (3 December 1713). It cannot be determined if Steele's authorship of *Robinson Crusoe* was assumed by the other members of the *Monitor* circle. The French edition owned by both the king and Ignacy Krasicki did not feature the name of Defoe as the author, while the publishing details of "*Robinson Crusoe* en anglois" (the entry for the English edition) are unknown. This is yet another piece of evidence that for the most of the eighteenth century the fame of Robinson did not add to the fame of its actual author.[30]

Then, concluding the preface, Albertrandi refers to the French afterlife of the novel, writing that notwithstanding the praise it received, it was criticised for the lengthy and "useless" remarks irritating the impatient readers (xii). This held especially for the third volume, which was full of "unrelated, random remarks", with no merits at all, spoiling the general impression. The critical remark is not linked with any names, but the obvious point of reference seems to have been Rousseau. There appeared a "general demand", Albertrandi writes, that someone "polishes the imperfections", a task that was eventually performed by Mr Feutry, who abbreviated the novel into two decent volumes, preserving "everything worth reading" (xiii). Apart from the *Serious Reflections* volume, the notable cuts included Crusoe's diary, merchant-like summaries, and most of Friday's religious education and the christening of his people. These could be explained by the intellectual trends promoted by the French Enlightenment philosophers. As such the novel merited a translation into Polish, which, the translator hopes, will be well received just as the other "more serious" (xiv) educational pieces he authored.

The publication of the first Polish translation of *Robinson Crusoe* was accompanied by related reviews published in some of the most important periodicals. The French-language *Journal Polonais* was focused on the books published by Michał Gröll, and accordingly, in Volume 3 there is a review of Feutry's edition, most probably copied from a relevant French journal.[31] *Wiadomości Warszawskie* (*Warsaw News*, 1769, 73/13 IX) features an advertisement written by Gröll himself: "The Adventures of Robinson Crusoe merit a Polish edition. Apart from the dominant romance element, which keeps the reader interested throughout, the book makes for a wonderful treatise on natural education".[32] The advertisement thus relates to two important aspects of the critical discourse of the 1760s in Poland: the anti-romance tendencies, still dependent on taxonomical inconsistencies ("romance" is seen as tantamount to adventures), and the possible, indirect benefits to reading fiction, here clearly by alluding to Rousseau. As such, the advertisement joins Albertrandi's preface in the attempt to distinguish *Robinson Crusoe* from the romance by virtue of its educational potential.

The second and third editions of Albertrandi's translation in 1774 and 1775, respectively, indicate a relatively lively publishing life – by Polish eighteenth-century standards, that is. The editions were printed by Łukasz Szlichtyn from Lwów (today Lviv), whose publishing house operated under a special privilege granted by King Stanislaus.[33] The information about the privilege is introduced in the title page, which apart from legitimising the publisher's ventures, indirectly exudes an aura of royal consent given for the further establishment of *Robinson Crusoe* in Stanislavian literary culture.

In 1775 Szlichtyn also published a relatively prompt Polish translation (anonymous) of *Naufrage et aventures de M. Pierre Viaud* (The Shipwreck and Adventures of Mr Pierre Viaud, 1768) – a very popular Robinsonade in 1770s Europe, today attributed to Jean Gaspard Dubois-Fontanelle. It would have been known by Krasicki, though the author of *Nicholas Wisdom* is unlikely to have been inspired by such scenes as Viaud devouring the "Friday" figure and preparing smoked chops as provisions. On the other hand, the transformation of the Robinson figure into a "savage", a structural move already implied in book IV of Swift's *Gulliver's Travels* as a form of indirect criticism of *Crusoe*'s positivism,[34] testified to the anxieties of the age, which would have been recognised by Krasicki, too: his Robinson/Nicholas, when confronted with the Nipuan utopia, also finds himself in the position of Friday.

By 1776, when *Nicholas Wisdom* was published, *Robinson Crusoe* had already established itself in the Stanislavian literary life. It is not surprising, in the light of the international afterlife of Defoe's novel, that its reception in Poland, on the one hand, was "authorless" – with no awareness of the actual author figure – and, on the other, had many agents: the king and his cultural reforms; the publishers and the translator coming from the royal circle; the French translator, who provided the source text; Rousseau, who determined its content and the manner of reading that transcended the confines of literature; Richard Steele, the alleged author, who metaphorically brought the novel closer to the aesthetic norms promoted in literary periodicals; and finally the fictitious Pierre Viaud, who exposed the generative potential of the Robinsonade pattern. When Krasicki worked on *Nicholas Wisdom* and *History*, this pattern was not part of a literary history told through names of authors and their output. Rather, it had already become part of what Gérard Genette calls the architext – a transcendent textual network out of which any new literary work emerges.[35] It had become an orphaned paradigm, deprived of the fatherlike author, and thus welcoming new ways of adoption and appropriation; a potential vehicle for new meanings, particularly suited to a reading culture that appreciated fictional travels, adventures and sentimentalised uses of nature. The several years framed by the appearance of *Robinson Crusoe* in Poland and Krasicki's employment of the Robinsonade pattern illustrate the emergence of a new literary culture in the Stanislavian Age: a dynamic network of connections, involving politics, book market, and periodical production. In this modern literary sphere, in a manner similar to what had been happening in England from the beginning of the eighteenth century, texts often lived lives of their own, disconnected from their authors. The *Robinson Crusoe* received in 1760s and 1770s Poland may not have been exactly what Daniel Defoe had written, but indeed the distance between Defoe's novel and its adaptations has been what has catalysed the development of the Robinsonade as a genre in the past 300 years.

Notes

Research for this chapter was funded by Narodowe Centrum Nauki, grant Miniatura II (2018/02/X/HS2/03216). An earlier version was first published as: Jakub Lipski, "Setting the Scene for the Polish Robinsonade: *The Adventures of Mr. Nicholas Wisdom* (1776) by Ignacy Krasicki and the Early Reception of Robinson Crusoe in Poland, 1769–1775", in *Rewriting Crusoe: The Robinsonade across Languages, Cultures, and Media*, ed. Jakub Lipski (Lewisburg: Bucknell University Press, 2020), 52–64.

1 The novel has been translated into English, and I am using the English title proposed by the translator, though a more accurate translation would be "Nicholas Experience". See Ignacy Krasicki, *The Adventures of Mr. Nicholas Wisdom*, trans. Thomas H. Hoisington (Evanston, IL: Northwestern University Press, 1992).
2 See Mieczysław Klimowicz, "Wstęp", in Ignacy Krasicki, *Mikołaja Doświadczyńskiego przypadki*, ed. Mieczysław Klimowicz (Wrocław: Zakład

Narodowy im. Ossolińskich, 1975), xxiv–xxxi. All quotations from the novel as well as other Polish sources are given in my translation.

3 See Czesław Miłosz, *The History of Polish Literature* (Berkeley: University of California Press, 1983), 177.

4 The romance-novel dialectic, as elaborated upon by Ian P. Watt in *The Rise of the Novel* (1957; repr., Berkeley: University of California Press, 2000), has been for at least three decades taken with a pinch of salt in English studies. See, especially, Margaret Anne Doody, *The True History of the Novel* (New Brunswick, NJ: Rutgers University Press, 1996). Admittedly, it appears to have enjoyed a longer life in Polish literary criticism. See Paweł Bohuszewicz, *Od "romansu" do powieści: Studia o polskiej literaturze narracyjnej (druga połowa XVII wieku – pierwsza połowa XIX wieku)* (Toruń: Wydawnictwo Naukowe Uniwersytetu Mikołaja Kopernika, 2016).

5 Krasicki, *Mikołaja Doświadczyńskiego przypadki*, 132.

6 Not that there is a clear-cut boundary between these two genres. See Artur Blaim, *Robinson Crusoe and His Doubles: The English Robinsonade of the Eighteenth Century* (Frankfurt: Peter Lang, 2016).

7 A useful evaluation of Krasicki's reliance on *Robinson Crusoe* and *Gulliver's Travels* is offered in Zofia Sinko, *Powieść angielska osiemnastego wieku a powieść polska lat, 1764–1830* (Warszawa: Państwowy Instytut Wydawniczy, 1961), 62–65.

8 Jadwiga Ruszała published two monographs on the Robinsonade in Poland: *Robinson w literaturze polskiej* [Robinson in Polish literature] (Słupsk: Wydawnictwo Wyższej Szkoły Pedagogicznej w Słupsku, 1998) and *Robinsonada w literaturze polskiej* [The Robinsonade in Polish literature] (Słupsk: Wydawnictwo Akademii Pomorskiej w Słupsku, 2000). Her work offers a useful overview of the phenomenon, especially in the nineteenth century and the first half of the twentieth. She includes *Nicholas Wisdom* in her list of quasi-Robinsonades but does not comment on the novel beyond briefly noting that it is an example of a utopia with a Robinsonade element.

9 See Elżbieta Dąbrowicz, "Syndrom rozbitka. Robinson Crusoe i Julian Ursyn Niemcewicz", *Porównania* 25.2 (2019): 21–42.

10 Ignacy Krasicki, *Historia* (Kraków: Universitas, 2002), 119.

11 Krasicki, *Historia*, 119.

12 See Klimowicz, "Wstęp", xxvii.

13 Jan IJ. van der Meer, *Literary Activities and Attitudes in the Stanislavian Age in Poland (1764–1795): A Social System?* (Amsterdam: Rodopi, 2002), 60. This number shows that studies of Enlightenment "print culture" in Poland should recognize the difference between Poland's fledgling literary market and what was happening in England at the same time.

14 Van der Meer, *Literary Activities and Attitudes*, 61.

15 See, for example, Nina Taylor-Terlecka, "Ossian in Poland", in *The Reception of Ossian in Europe*, ed. Howard Gaskill (London: Thoemmes Continuum, 2004), 240–258 and Grażyna Bystydzieńska and Wojciech Nowicki, "Sterne in Poland", in *The Reception of Laurence Sterne in Europe*, ed. Peter de Voogd and John Neubauer (London: Thoemmes Continuum, 2004), 154–164.

16 Richard Butterwick, *Poland's Last King and English Culture: Stanisław August Poniatowski, 1732–1798* (Oxford: Clarendon, 1998), 182.

17 Krasicki's library, including several thousand items, was one of the biggest collections among the Polish nobility. For the inventory, see Sante Graciotti

and Jadwiga Rudnicka (eds.), *Inwentarz biblioteki Ignacego Krasickiego z 1810 r* (Wrocław: Zakład Narodowy im. Ossolińskich, 1973).

18 Jadwiga Rudnicka (ed.), *Biblioteka Stanisława Augusta na Zamku Warszawskim: Dokumenty, Archiwum Literackie* 26 (1988): 67–83.

19 See Chapter 4 of Butterwick, *Poland's Last King* ("The Influence of Sir Charles Hanbury Williams"), 86–101.

20 Zofia Sinko, "Powieść zachodnioeuropejska w Polsce stanisławowskiej na podstawie inwentarzy bibliotecznych i katalogów", *Pamiętnik Literacki* 57.4 (1966): 581–624.

21 Dorota Żołądź-Strzelczyk, "Kilka uwag o znajomości dzieła Jana Jakuba Rousseau *Emil, czyli o wychowaniu* w Polsce przełomu XVIII i XIX wieku", *Problemy wczesnej edukacji* 2.29 (2015): 7–14.

22 Klimowicz, "Wstęp", xlii–xliii.

23 "Editions in French and Some Other Translations", in *Robinson Crusoe at Yale. Yale University Library Gazette* 11.2 (1936): 28–32.

24 As Sinko points out, Feutry's version was in fact an adaptation/abbreviation of the already existent 1721 translation by Saint-Hyacinthe. Sinko, *Powieść angielska*, 19.

25 Jean-Jacques Rousseau, *Emile, or On Education*, ed. and trans. Christopher Kelly and Allan Bloom (Hanover, NH: University Press of New England, 2010), 332.

26 Rousseau, *Emile*, 332.

27 "It is Rousseau who begins Crusoe's life as a hero of specifically childhood reading". Teresa Michals, *Books for Children, Books for Adults: Age and the Novel from Defoe to James* (Cambridge: Cambridge University Press, 2014), 38.

28 Quoted after Ruszała, *Robinson w literaturze polskiej*, 30.

29 [Daniel Defoe], *Przypadki Robinsona Krusoe*, trans. Jan Chrzciciel Albertrandi (Warszawa: Nakładem Michała Grela, 1769). Further references are to this edition and are given parenthetically.

30 Throughout the eighteenth century, Defoe was not considered to be part of the new novelistic tradition. For a study of this phenomenon and the change ushered in by Walter Scott's appreciation of Defoe, see Homer Obed Brown, "The Institution of the English Novel: Defoe's Contribution", *Novel: A Forum on Fiction* 29.3 (1996): 299–318.

31 *Journal Polonais* 3 (1769): 81–85. See Ruszała, *Robinson w literaturze polskiej*, 29.

32 Quoted after Ruszała, *Robinson w literaturze polskiej*, 29.

33 Maria Juda, "Uprzywilejowane drukarnie we Lwowie doby staropolskiej", *Folia Bibliologica* 55/56 (2013/2014): 16–17. For the third edition, Szlichtyn preserved the details of the first edition, including Michał Gröll's name as publisher, in the preliminary pages.

34 This tension is nevertheless present in *Robinson Crusoe*, too. Robinson repeatedly expresses his anxiety over becoming a "beast", while in *The Farther Adventures* "the young Woman" whom Robinson saves thus recounts the hunger she experienced when on board the ship: "had my Mistress been dead, as much as I lov'd her, I am certain, I should have eaten a Piece of her Flesh". Daniel Defoe, *The Farther Adventures of Robinson Crusoe*, ed. W. R. Owens (London: Routledge, 2017), 117.

35 Gérard Genette, *The Architext: An Introduction* (Berkeley: University of California Press, 1992).

4 Izabela Czartoryska (1746–1835) as Reader and Promoter of Sterne

In the last two decades, the reception of Laurence Sterne in Poland has been given some critical attention (with several essays published in the English language),[1] even if a comprehensive account of the phenomenon, comparable to the achievements of German and French Sterneans, has yet to be written.[2] This chapter contributes to this recent "Sterne in Poland" criticism by offering a close evaluation of the cultural and literary ventures of Princess Izabela Czartoryska, the hostess of the celebrated Puławy circle and arguably the finest of Poland's early Sterneans. Sterne was one of the shortlisted authors on Princess Czartoryska's reading list, and the extant evidence of the manner in which she responded to both *A Sentimental Journey* and *Tristram Shandy*, including letters, commonplace book excerpts, as well as an attempt at translation, suggests that she would have contributed substantially to the Sternean fashions in Poland in the decades to come. As a rule, critics are more attentive to Sternean influences on Maria Wirtemberska's work, but it was Princess Izabela (Wirtemberska's mother) who recommended Sterne's *A Sentimental Journey* to her daughter, and who merits attention as the one who orientated Sterne readings in late eighteenth- and early nineteenth-century Poland.

English Literature in Puławy at the Turn of the Eighteenth Century

In order to contextualise properly the Sternean interests of Czartoryska, some remarks must be made on the literary fashions in the Puławy circle. Princess Izabela (neé Flemming) Czartoryska and her husband Prince Adam Kazimierz Czartoryski, members of the patriotic and cultural elite of Warsaw, moved to rural Puławy in Eastern Poland in 1785. Their decision to relocate was both politically and ideologically motivated. On the one hand, it was a reaction against the policies of King Stanislaus August, which eventually led to the partitions of Poland; on the other, it

DOI: 10.4324/9781003153016-7

was influenced by contemporary fashions for criticising the metropolis and extolling life in the countryside characterised by authentic contact with nature.[3] Puławy soon became a cultural centre of the gradually partitioned Poland, and the Czartoryskis would prove generous hosts to those literary and artistic types who would help them realise their patriotic and intellectual programme

Both Prince Adam Kazimierz and Princess Izabela were avid readers of English imaginative and factual literature, and were largely inspired by what they would call "the English way of life". Their Anglophilia can be explained not only by a general turn to things English in the Poland of King Stanislaus, but also by Prince Adam Kazimierz's Scottish ancestry – his predecessors were related to the Gordon clan in seventeenth-century Scotland. Their fondness for England and Scotland would have also been shaped and reinforced during their several journeys to the British Isles. For the purposes of this chapter, there is no need to draw a detailed outline of the multi-faceted English inspirations the Czartoryskis derived, including those coming from such diverse spheres as gardening, architecture, design, cuisine, clothing, education or political and economic thought. These are duly discussed by Zofia Gołębiowska in her monograph study of "English influences in Puławy".[4] What will suffice here is a brief discussion of the role of English literature in the intellectual life of the circle. The Czartoryskis and their guests were predominantly interested in more or less contemporary English literature, thus manifesting their fashionability. The most popular genre in the Puławy circle was the novel, and the most notable examples ranged from works by Daniel Defoe, Henry Fielding and Tobias Smollett to those by Samuel Richardson, Oliver Goldsmith and finally Laurence Sterne.[5] Apart from the early English novel, the Czartoryski circle delighted in the late eighteenth- and early nineteenth-century Gothic, especially in the works of Ann Radcliffe and Matthew Gregory Lewis, as well as in the realist writings of Maria Edgeworth and Jane Austen. Another highly influential author within the circle was Walter Scott, who even exchanged letters with Adam Konstanty, the son of Prince Adam Kazimierz and Princess Izabela. As for English poetry, the fashions in Puławy also largely corresponded to those elsewhere on the Continent. Authors read and admired included John Milton, Alexander Pope, James Thomson, Edward Young and later Lord Byron. The Czartoryskis were also swept up in the ossianic craze in contemporary Europe, with Princess Izabela being a staunch defender of the songs' authenticity. Finally, the Puławy circle played a significant role in the eighteenth-century re-discovery of Shakespeare in Poland and orientated Shakespearean reception in Poland for years to come. The Czartoryskis' fascination with the Bard led them to collect souvenirs associated with the dramatist, such as the so-called "Shakespeare's chair" or a remnant of a mulberry tree he had allegedly planted.

Some of the predilections above would have been formed or reinforced on Izabela's "Tour through England", as she herself labels her 1789–1791 travels in England and Scotland in the company of her son. The tour was originally to have been her son's educational journey, and thus the account of it, written in French, abounds in factual content, with issues ranging from economy and industry to law and politics. Nevertheless, the manuscript is also testimony to Czartoryska's acquaintance with the contemporary conventions of picturesque and literary tourism, with much space devoted to landscape and architectural sketches and descriptions of places holding literary connotations. Alina Aleksandrowicz even compares the narrative persona of the princess with Sterne's Mr Yorick and his preoccupation with nature,[6] though it seems a rather far-fetched juxtaposition.

Sternean Fashions in Puławy

Even though Laurence Sterne was only one of several major authors enjoyed in Puławy, and though his impact on the literary life of the Czartoryski circle was by no means as powerful as that of Shakespeare, Princess Izabela seems to have felt a special predilection for him. In 1782, she wrote a letter to the French poet Jacques Delille asking for an inscription for a pyramid memorial she planned to accommodate in her garden. Sterne's name was to be included there as one of those who were associated with "sensibility, cordial memories and gratitude".[7] Czartoryska added that everyone in their estate was preoccupied with erecting this monument, and that the authors who were to be commemorated were "not only teachers but also sources of pleasure and feeling".[8] This is the context in which Sterne's name appeared:

> On one side there will be Pope, Milton, Young, Sterne, Shakespeare, Racine and Rousseau; on the other one, Petrarch, Anacreon, Metastasio, Tasso and Lafontaine; on the third, Mrs. Sévignié, Ricobini, La Fayette, Desouliers and Sapho; finally, on the fourth, Virgil, Gessner, Gresset and Delille. Each side of the pyramid shall be ornamented by trees, shrubs and flowers.[9]

The project was eventually not realised, most probably due to Delille's high opinion of himself and lack of enthusiasm about being listed among a number of names. In his answer to Princess Izabela, the poet suggested that marbles do not go very well with natural scenery, and that so far he had been, as a rule, commemorated by newly planted trees named after him (exclusively after him, one could add).[10] Never-theless, the project does indicate that the Sternean interests of Princess Izabela had been developing even before the Czartoryskis finally settled in the estate in 1785.[11] As a result, Sterne had been read and appre-ciated in the Puławy circle several decades before he was widely acclaimed by the Polish Romantics in the 1820s and early 1830s. The Czartoryskis would collect Sterne's books in original versions and in French translation in their library.[12] In a manner similar to con-temporary Sterneans in Germany (such as the Lorenzo Order), the members of the Puławy circle would treat these texts, especially the *Sermons*, the *Journey* and selected correspondence, as conduct books advocating practical implications of the cult of feeling. It was common to address close friends by the name of Yorick. Small gifts were deco-rated with the sentimental traveller's portrait, which custom seems to have been modelled on the Lorenzo Order's quasi-ritualistic practice of exchanging snuff boxes. Drawing upon the *Journey* and *Sermons*, the Czartoryski circle followed a Sternean ethical code, advocating such values as philanthropy, friendship, strong emotional bonds, sensitivity and sensibility, which again suggests the influence of the German order.[13] As a rule, readers at Puławy seem to have taken Sterne's sen-timentalism at face value, missing his ironic modelling of gesture and erotic undertones.[14] In this they followed the patterns of Sternean reception on the Continent, most notably in Germany, France and Russia. It is worth adding here that the cult of feeling in Poland, to which the readings of Sterne contributed substantially, was part of a larger socio-cultural programme undertaken by the Polish aristocratic elites, aiming at instilling in Poles the current fashions on the Con-tinent (especially in France and Germany) and in Britain, with the intention of turning what they understood as the nation's narrow-mindedness into modern cosmopolitanism.

As mentioned before, the Czartoryskis surrounded themselves with those who shared their interests. One of them was the French artist Jean-Pierre Norblin (1745–1830), who moved to Poland in 1774 in order to become the family's court painter. Norblin's Watteau-like style made him a good fit for Princess Izabela's sentimental programme, first in Warsaw in the Powązki Estate and then in Puławy. He was also an occasional book illustrator, and in 1794 his attention was drawn to *Tristram Shandy*. The only extant testimony to the artist's Shandean endeavours is the drawing "Alas Poor Yorick" (Figure 4.1).

Another figure rubbing shoulders with the Czartoryskis was Fran-ciszek Salezy Jezierski, a rather unsuccessful writer who in the year 1790 published a political pamphlet criticising Poland's government.

Figure 4.1 Jean-Pierre Norblin, "Illustration to Tristram Shandy", 1794. Inventory number: XV-Rr.1021. Property of the National Museum in Cracow/The Czartoryski Museum in Cracow.

Curiously enough, the piece pretended to have been written by "Mr Sterne", a fact which is illustrative of the tendency to politicise Sterne's text in Puławy.[15]

Tutor to Izabela's children, Krystyn Lach Szyrma, was also an open admirer of Sterne. He was the guide of young Adam Konstanty Czartoryski during his journey to Great Britain, and, appropriately enough, kept a travel journal when on the road. According to the account, they whiled away their sojourn in Calais at Dessein's, reading *A Sentimental Journey*, which "outshines so many other works", and *Tristram Shandy*, which "even some English readers find difficult to comprehend".[16]

Finally, Princess Izabela inspired her daughter Mary (later Princess Mary von Württemberg, in Polish – Maria Wirtemberska), who not only relied on Sternean sentimental ethics but also attempted to imitate Sterne's literary methods in her novel *Malvina, or the Heart's Intuition*

(1816) and the travelogue *Niektóre zdarzenia, myśli i uczucia doznane za granicą* [Some occurrences, thoughts and emotions experienced abroad] (1816–1818, published in 1978).[17]

Princess Izabela's Sternean Miscellanies

Apart from the mention of Sterne in Czartoryska's letter to Delille, the first more extensive Sternean document is the princess's letter to her daughter Mary (dated 5 February 1784), in which Czartoryska brings "Voyage sentimental" to the other's attention.[18] Given her daughter's literary career in the years to come, the letter should be considered as a substantial contribution to Sterne's reception in Poland. Izabela's recommendation must have triggered her daughter's interest in Sterne, which would later result in Wirtemberska's own "journey of the heart". As a matter of fact, however, Princess Izabela herself toyed with the idea of writing a "sentimental journey". Several decades later, she openly expressed her plan in a letter to her husband (dated 3 July 1811):

> Having gathered my thoughts, I started to write something which I cannot yet properly name … It is devoted to a former cavalry captain from Pokucie, who has lived for some time in the countryside. At one point his doctors prescribe him the Carlsbad waters so that he would recover after an illness. After describing his person, life, habits, home and way of thinking, I send him on the road with two servants. Passing Lviv, Tarnów, Cracow and Prague, he arrives in Carlsbad. Having finished with the waters, he comes home, passing Wrocław, Greater Poland and Warsaw. *Ces't me … voyage sentimental.* [19]

The letter is evidence of a continuous interest in *A Sentimental Journey*, as well as of the awareness that the term "sentimental journey" began to be understood generically, but also an indication of Czartoryska's acquaintance with *Tristram Shandy*. There is something inherently Shandean about describing the traveller's "person, life, habits, home and way of thinking", and thus suspending the progress of the travel narrative. Though the plan of a fictional sentimental journey was eventually not realised, five years later Princess Izabela penned a diary of her own stagecoach travel to Bad Warmbrunn (*Dyliżansem przez Śląsk* [Stagecoach across Silesia], 1816, published in 1968). The travelogue is a rather curious piece of writing, constituted by a peculiar patchwork of literary conventions testifying to Princess Izabela's readings and interests. It has some qualities of an "impersonal relating of facts", as Charles Batten labelled the tradition of objective accounts in the first half of the eighteenth century,[20] but is also indebted to the late eighteenth-century vogue for picturesque tours, given the abundance of well-written land-scape descriptions relying on the categories of the picturesque and the sublime. More importantly, however, it is also characterised by some openly Sternean allusions. If reports of compulsive, as it were, alms giving and tear shedding can be taken as part of Princess Izabela's sentimental ethos, not necessarily related to a single literary source, her attention to seemingly irrelevant details should by all means be related to *A Senti-mental Journey*. How else to explain the entry for July 6, where she recounts purchasing a pair of fine goatskin gloves in the context of her participation in a folk festival?

> It all happened in a beautiful and joyful neighbourhood, and the exceptional atmosphere of sincerity, joy and merriment were testi-mony to prosperity and good humour. This situation filled my heart with the kind of inward bliss I feel whenever I see happy and contented people. We spent the night in Świdnica. The next day, before leaving, we bought decent and well made gloves. The man-ufacturer declared that they had been made of goatskin and that he sells 16 000 dozens yearly with ease.[21]

Unlike her daughter Maria, Princess Izabela was rather indifferent to Sternean punctuation, which can also be seen in the way she noted extracts from *Tristram Shandy* and *A Sentimental Journey* (as I will demonstrate later on). I would argue, though, that the plausible sources of inspiration for the passage above are the "children of Nature" and "grisette" episodes from *A Sentimental Journey* respectively.

It has been generally assumed in Polish criticism of "Sterne in Poland" that *A Sentimental Journey* exerted a much more powerful influence on the sentimentally predisposed readers in turn-of-the-century Poland. Bystyd-zieńska and Nowicki go so far as to claim that at the time "only ASJ was known and read".[22] As a matter of fact, *Tristram Shandy* was by all means read at the court of King Stanislaus August, and this is where the Czar-toryskis might have had early contact with the text. The king's familiarity with the novel is recorded in the memoirs of his librarian Marc Reverdil, who relates being asked by his sovereign to deliver an out-loud reading of *Tristram Shandy* in English.[23] Explicit evidence of Princess Izabela's acquaintance with Sterne's opus magnum is to be found in her three-volume *Extraits*, on which she worked continuously from the early 1790s.

The first volume gathers excerpts from chronicles and history books, while the second is made up of representative passages coming from var-ious notable texts. The later third volume (dated 1809) is for the most part a revised selection of the second one. The two Shandean entries in the second volume were added around the year 1795 (judging by the context of what precedes and what follows – the entries themselves are not dated). The first one is a reflection on the passing of time from Volume 9, Chapter 8, while the second explores how "Stillness", "Silence" and "Listlessness" comfort the troubled mind of Uncle Toby in the aftermath of a fervent discussion on the demolition of Dunkirk (Volume 9, Chapter 35). The excerpts are in French and would have been adapted (rather than quoted word for word) from the 1785 French translation by Charles-François de Bonnay, though the edition is not to be found in the Czartoryski collection today, and Princess Izabela did not provide any reference to her source. The two excerpts are preceded by a quote from Milton (a description of the evening) and one from Shakespeare (a description of the morning), both of which correspond to the time-oriented quotes from Sterne. In both excerpts Czartoryska introduces some changes, which are by no means limited to punctuation. The first one is made more personal, with the recollection of Jenny exchanged for the princess's daughter ("ma chere Enfant"), and the concluding remark on "eternal separation" modified into "separation si longue".[24] The second passage, in turn, is deprived of any mention of Dunkirk or Uncle Toby, and his solitary cabinet becomes the princess's own place of retreat:

C'est ainsi qu'un ou deux entretiens de ce genre avec Trim sur la demolition de Dunckerque, — entretiens charmans, mais trop courts! — rappellèrent pour un moment à mon oncle Tobie le souvenir des plaisirs qu'il avoit perdus. ... — La magie avoit disparu; & l'ame de mon oncle Tobie avoit perdu son resort. — Le calme accompagné du silence avoit pénétré dans le cabinet solitaire de mon oncle Tobie. — Ils avoient étendu leurs voiles de gaze sur sa tête; & l'indifférence, au regard vague & à la fibre lâche, s'étoit assise tranquillement à ses côtés. —[25]

Souvent des entretiens charmans, mais helas! Trop courts, me rappellent pour quelques moments, le souvenir des plaisirs qui j'ai perdu: ... La magie est disparue, et l'ame a perdue son resort. Le calme accompagne du Silence a penetré dans meu cabinet Solitairre, ils ont etendus leurs voiles legers sur ma tete et & l'indifference aux regards vagues, et aux fibres laches, s'est assise tranquillement a mes cotés.[26]

Czartoryska's technique of de-contextualising the pieces by eliminating proper names on the one hand dissociates the quotes from Shandean intricacies and, on the other one, makes them more universal and open to new interpretations. The princess's choice of fragments and her manner of adaptation were by no means accidental. The excerpts are illustrative of the tendency in Puławy to read Sterne sentimentally and politically, and the most probable date of the entries relates them to the second and third partition of Poland. The first entry creates a melancholic atmosphere of evanescence, while the second expresses a longing for tranquillity, the lack of which is painfully experienced by a mind troubled by history. This arrangement would have certainly appealed to the Polish patriots lamenting the lot of their motherland. Princess Izabela's decision to rewrite the two passages in the third volume of her *Extraits* [27] is testimony to their unwavering significance to her. Arguably, Czartoryska was the most patriotically predisposed member of the Puławy circle, and her voice was a strong and respected one. She set the example of a melancholic *penserosa*, thoughtful of the turbulent downfall of her country.

Another Sternean specimen which continued to be close to Czartoryska's heart was the apostrophe to liberty from the starling episode in *A Sentimental Journey*. The tendency to read Sterne as promoter of freedom was a Polish peculiarity at the time, and it has been discussed in detail by others.[28] In the late eighteenth century the country was gradually partitioned by its neighbours, Russia, Austria and Prussia, and one of the popular forms of socio-cultural activism on the part of the patriotic elite was promotion of appropriate reading habits. It is impossible to determine with any degree of certainty whether this reception of *A Sentimental Journey* originated in Princess Izabela's readings of Sterne, but the fact that she highlighted the apostrophe to liberty would not have gone unnoticed in the Puławy circle. The earliest evidence of her fondness for the episode can be found in the second volume of *Extraits*, where she rewrote the fragment from Frénais's translation.[29] This time Czartoryska faithfully copied the text, introducing only minor punctuation and lexical changes with no real agenda, and shortening it to some extent. The entry appears shortly after the Shandean ones, and thus it would have served the same purpose of expressing Izabela's anxieties at the time of the partition of Poland.

Princess Izabela elaborated on Sterne's notion of liberty in her *Katalog pamiątek złożonych w Domu Gotyckim w Puławach* [Catalogue of Souvenirs from the Gothic House in Puławy] from 1809. Adopting the same technique of de-contextualisation, Czartoryska translates the apostrophe into Polish and then re-contextualises the piece using it as the beginning of her essay devoted to the Swiss champion of freedom William Tell, which was to serve as a commentary to "Tell's arrow" exhibited in the Gothic House, one of the chief venues for the display of the princess's programme within the Puławy estate. Combining

Sterne's appreciation of liberty with an embodiment of the fight for national independence conveyed an obviously clear political message, aimed at rejuvenating the patriotic sentiments of visitors to Puławy. Czartoryska's adaptation of the fragment is also revealing of her conservative standpoint: the princess does not absolutise liberty and dares to correct Sterne's text. Her translation of the original "till NATURE herself shall change"[30] is accompanied with the remark "or your laws shall be wrongly used".[31] As Aleksandrowicz points out, the added reservation stemmed from Czartoryska's aversion to the French Revolution.[32] In fact, Czartoryska herself concludes her translation with a suitable commentary:

> These are the words with which Stern [sic], the famous English author, painted the beauties of blissful liberty. He did not foresee the bitter fruits this liberty bore all over the world at the end of the 18th century, when frantic ambitions had no respect for her limits.[33]

Sterne's text, then, is not only arbitrarily de-contextualised, in line with the tendency to read him sentimentally, but also "improved" in accord with Czartoryska's rather aristocratic understanding of freedom. Proceeding to introduce the figure of Tell, the princess explains her use of the passage from Sterne by its potential to evoke the nostalgic longing for the past of "restrained liberty" (*umiarkowana wolność*), which she associates with William Tell.[34] Czartoryska's patriotic programme, which included a peculiar reading of Sterne, was thus not about kindling revolutionary fervour in Poles, as would be the case with the first generation of Polish Romantics. Rather, it was constituted by a melancholic reflection on what was lost.

On the whole, Princess Izabela Czartoryska's Sternean miscellanies can be approached in two ways: either as trend setters or only as testimonies to the fashions in the Puławy circle. In an attempt to solve this "chicken or egg"-like dilemma, I would like to point out that practically all the texts, even those which were seemingly confined to the private sphere, went to the public and were meant to be read, notwithstanding the manuscript form. This was even the case with the *Extraits,* the third volume of which was displayed in the Gothic House. I would argue then that even if Princess Izabela did not produce a Sternean literary output comparable to that of her daughter Maria Wirtemberska, her inspirational role in recognising in Sterne those aspects that matched the aesthetic tastes and political concerns of late eighteenth-century Poland should be duly acknowledged.

Notes

An earlier version of this chapter was first published as: Jakub Lipski, "Poland's Finest Sternean: Izabela Czartoryska (1746–1835) as Reader and Promoter of Sterne", *The Shandean* 27 (2016): 9–25.

1 Natalia Rezmer-Mrówczyńska, "Sterne in Poland in the Age of the Enlightenment", *The Shandean* 24 (2013): 119–120; Grażyna Bystydzieńska and Wojciech Nowicki, "Sterne in Poland", in *The Reception of Laurence Sterne in Europe*, ed. Peter de Voogd and John Neubauer (London: Continuum, 2004), 154–164; Grażyna Bystydzieńska, "Wawrzyniec Sterne: *A Sentimental Journey* in 19th Century Poland", *The Shandean* 13 (2002): 47–53; Wojciech Nowicki, "An Anachronistic Hoax", *The Shandean* 13 (2002): 106–109.

2 See, for example, Lana Asfour, *Laurence Sterne in France* (London: Continuum, 2008) and Klaus Vieweg, James Vigus and Kathleen M. Wheeler (eds.), *Shandean Humour in English and German Literature and Philosophy* (Oxford: Legenda, 2017).

3 Zofia Gołębiowska, *W kręgu Czartoryskich: Wpływy angielskie w Puławach na przełomie XVIII i XIX wieku* [In the Czartoryskis' circle: English influences in Puławy at the turn of the eighteenth century] (Lublin: Wydawnictwo Uniwersytetu Marii Curie-Skłodowskiej, 2000), 160.

4 See Gołębiowska, *W kręgu Czartoryskich*; basic issues are also presented in her article in English: Zofia Gołębiowska, "British Models and Inspirations in Czartoryskis' Country Residence in Puławy at the Turn of the Eighteenth Century", in *Culture at Global/Local Levels: British and Commonwealth Contribution to World Civilisation*, ed. Krystyna Kujawińska-Courtney (Łódź: Wydawnictwo Biblioteka, 2002), 139–150.

5 Basing her judgement on the correspondence of the Puławy circle, though not giving any detailed references, Gołębiowska suggests that the first three authors were enjoyed largely by men, whereas the latter group provided entertainment for the female members. This gendered view of the reading habits in Puławy may indeed throw some light on Princess Izabela's role in promoting Sternean fashions, but it should not be taken for granted. Izabela's *Extraits* [Extracts from literature] abound in Fieldingesque quotations, whereas some of the many volumes of *Tristram Shandy* collected in the Czartoryski library were annotated by Prince Adam Kazimierz. See Gołębiowska, *W kręgu Czartoryskich*, 165–167.

6 Alina Aleksandrowicz, *Izabela Czartoryska: Polskość i europejskość* [Izabela Czartoryska: Polishness and Europeanness] (Lublin: Wydawnictwo Uniwersytetu Marii Curie-Skłodowskiej, 1998), 186.

7 Quoted in Alojzy Feliński, *Ziemianin, czyli ziemiaństwo francuskie Jakuba Delille'a przez Alojzego Felińskiego wierszem polskim przełożone* [A Polish translation of Delille's L'homme des champs, ou Les géorgiques françaises] (Kraków, 1823), 138. The volume includes Czartoryska's letter to Delille, as well as his response, in Polish translation. All the translations from Polish into English in this chapter are mine. Please note that Czartoryska's idiosyncrasies of French and English spelling are retained.

8 Feliński, *Ziemianin*, 138.

9 Feliński, *Ziemianin*, 138–139.

10 Feliński, *Ziemianin*, 140–144.

11 Czartoryska would have become acquainted with Sterne already in Warsaw, being a member of the literary salon hosted by King Stanislaus, an avid Anglophile and Sternean, and Czartoryska's lover for some time. Czartoryska would then have acquainted herself with Sterne before the first edition of *The Beauties of Sterne* was published (1782); a fact pointing to a rather more authentic contact with *Tristram Shandy* and *A Sentimental Journey*.

12 As of today, the library contains three incomplete sets of *Tristram Shandy*: volumes 1 and 2 of the 1760 edition; volumes 2, 3, 4, 5, 6 of the 1770 edition; as well as volumes 4, 5, 6 of the 1782 edition. One way of explaining this rather surprising abundance would be by suggesting that they might have continuously attempted to obtain one complete set of all the volumes. Apart from *Tristram Shandy*, the library also holds *Letters from Yorick to Eliza* from 1775, Frénais's translation of A *Sentimental Journey* from 1789, the 1790 edition of *A Collection of Letters and Miscellaneous Writings* as well as *The Beauties of Sterne* from the same year.

13 Gołębiowska, *W kręgu Czartoryskich*, 169.

14 Accordingly, Polish nineteenth-century translations of *A Sentimental Journey* omit or tone down some of the most frivolous or "immoral" episodes. See Bystydzieńska and Nowicki, "Sterne in Poland", 160; Grażyna Bystydzieńska, "O polskich przekładach literatury angielskiej w XVIII wieku" [On the Polish translations of eighteenth-century English literature], *Wiek Oświecenia* [The Age of Enlightenment] 29 (2013): 108.

15 For a more detailed discussion, see Nowicki, "An Anachronistic Hoax"; and Bystydzieńska and Nowicki, "Sterne in Poland", 154–156.

16 Krystyn Lach Szyrma, *Anglia i Szkocja: Przypomnienie z podróży roku 1820–1824 odbytej* [England and Scotland: memories of a journey made in 1820–1824], ed. Paweł Hertz (Warszawa: Państwowy Instytut Wydawniczy, 1981), 14–15.

17 See Alina Aleksandrowicz, "Nieznana 'Podróż sentymentalna' Marii Wirtemberskiej" [Maria Wirtemberska's unknown "Sentimental Journey"], *Pamiętnik Literacki* 59.2 (1968): 5–39 and Magdalena Ożarska, "A Striking Reduction of the Visual: The Imaginative and the Familial Gaze in Maria Wirtemberska's *Niektóre zdarzenia, myśli i uczucia doznane za granicą* [Certain events, thoughts and feelings experienced abroad] (1816–1818)", *Studies in Travel Writing* 22.1 (2018): 61–62.

18 Izabela Czartoryska, Letter to her daughter Mary from 5 February 1784 (The Czartoryski Library in Cracow, MS 6137 II).

19 Izabela Czartoryska, Letter to her husband Adam Kazimierz from 3 July 1811 (The Czartoryski Library in Cracow, MS 6030 III), 91–92.

20 Charles L. Batten Jr., *Pleasurable Instruction: Form and Convention in Eighteenth-Century Travel Literature* (Berkeley: University of California Press, 1978), 41.

21 Izabela Czartoryska, *Dyliżansem przez Śląsk: Dziennik podróży do Cieplic w roku 1816* [Stagecoach across Silesia: Diary of a journey to Bad Warmbrunn in 1816] (Wrocław: Zakład Narodowy im. Ossolińskich, 1968), 52.

22 Bystydzieńska and Nowicki, "Sterne in Poland", 154.

23 See Zofia Sinko, *Powieść zachodnioeuropejska w kulturze literackiej polskiego Oświecenia* [The Western European novel in the literary culture of the Polish Enlightenment] (Wrocław: Zakład Narodowy im. Ossolińskich, 1968), 202.

24 Izabela Czartoryska, *Extraits*, vol. 2 (The Czartoryski Library in Cracow, MS 6070), 306. Czartoryska would have used the following edition of *Tristram Shandy*: Laurence Sterne, *Suite de la Vie et des opinions de Tristram Shandy*, vol. 2, trans. Charles-François de Bonnay (Paris: Volland, 1785), 217–218.

25 Sterne, *Suite de la Vie et des opinions de Tristram Shandy*, vol. 3, 312.

26 Czartoryska, *Extraits*, vol. 2, 306.

27 Czartoryska, *Extraits*, vol. 3, 191–192.

28 See, for example, Bystydzieńska and Nowicki, "Sterne in Poland", 154–156.

29 Czartoryska, *Extraits*, vol. 2, 309.

30 Laurence Sterne, *A Sentimental Journey through France and Italy* and *Continuation of the Bramine's Journal*, ed. Melvyn New and W.G. Day (Gainsville: University Press of Florida, 2002), 96.

31 Czartoryska's version reads "chyba Natura zmienny obrót weźmie albo prawa twoje na złe użyte będą". Izabela Czartoryska, "Strzała Tella", in *Katalog pamiątek złożonych w Domu Gotyckim w Puławach* [Catalogue of Souvenirs from the Gothic House in Puławy], vol. 3 (The Czartoryski Library in Cracow, MS 2917), 253.

32 Aleksandrowicz, *Izabela Czartoryska: Polskość i europejskość*, 156.

33 Czartoryska, "Strzała Tella", 253.

34 Czartoryska, "Strzała Tella", 253.

Part III

Critical Afterlives

5 Sterne's *A Sentimental Journey* and Contemporary Travel Writing Studies

We are clearly past the moment in literary studies when the author's words addressing his or her own work were taken for granted. On the other hand, much trust is still placed in Laurence Sterne's self-proclaimed novelty and to the extent that one may yield to a temptation to read Sterne as a revolutionary in prose fiction, travel writing, autobiography or sermon writing. Those who succumb to the temptation seem to forget that a claim for innovativeness was a common trope in eighteenth-century self-reflexive practices. Let us recall Henry Fielding and his preface to *Joseph Andrews* (1742),[1] Horace Walpole's remarks about originating "a new species of romance" in the preface to the second edition of *The Castle of Otranto* (1765),[2] or the bold statements of debuting Frances Burney distinguishing *Evelina* (1778) from the works of her predecessors.[3] Sterne was no different and advertised both *Tristram Shandy* (1759–1767) and *A Sentimental Journey* (1768) as highly original and, one could add, hitherto unattempted in the English language. As for the latter, Sterne's Yorick self-consciously underlines the "*Novelty of* [his] *Vehicle*", writing that "both [his] travels and observations will be altogether of a different cast from any of [his] fore-runners".[4] A similar remark about the *Journey*'s originality can be found in one of Sterne's letters addressed to his daughter: "I have laid a plan for something new, quite out of the beaten track".[5]

No Sternean would wish to undermine Sterne's achievements and deny him artistry. That said, the notions of revolution, broken grounds or turning points in literary criticism are often mere constructs that help organise critical discourse, especially literary history, and fail to address the complexities of literary production. Being too enthusiastic about Sterne's revolutions, one might lose sight of the immediate context and anachronistically relish his timelessness in the company of "fellow modernists" in prose fiction and "fellow Romanticists" in travel writing.

There have been attempts to dispel some of these myths of reception in Sterne studies. Thomas Keymer undermined the critical cliché that

DOI: 10.4324/9781003153016-9

Sterne's digressiveness and excessive self-consciousness in *Tristram Shandy* could be seen as his claim for originality. As he put it, "far from representing some radically original scrutiny of novelistic convention, self-referential gestures of this kind had become just another part of the convention".[6] Christopher Fanning, in turn, offered a contextualised discussion of Sterne's textuality, in which his experiments with the *mise-en-page* – a quality that is often taken to illustrate the writer's novelty – are seen as stemming from the Scriblerian tradition.[7] As for the sermons, they have been discussed as part of the Church of England's homiletic tradition and even labelled "statements of commonplace Anglican thought".[8] In general, Melvyn New and the other editors to the *Florida Edition of the Works of Laurence Sterne* (1978–2014) have done much to read Sterne as one writing in a particular milieu and in the context of his contemporaries and predecessors.

The case of travel writing studies appears to be different. Here, the "novelty of [Sterne's] vehicle" is all too often taken for granted. This is especially the case when Sterne himself is not the primary object of interest. A peripheral remark, a sketch of the background, a search for sources of inspiration – the introduction of Sterne and *A Sentimental Journey* tends to be more than convenient to corroborate the critical narrative. Thomas Curley's "Sterne's *A Sentimental Journey* and the tradition of travel literature"[9] makes for an apt summary of this critical tendency. Curley writes how in *A Sentimental Journey* Sterne adapted "geographic conventions inherited from the Renaissance and the Enlightenment to become an unprecedented travelogue of subjective spiritual exploration".[10] The thesis is supported by Sterne's own declaration that the narrative is "altogether of a different cast from any of my fore-runners" and a remark that the *Journey* anticipated "some of the best Romantic narratives of travel". Curley asserts that Sterne was very well read in travel literature and that Volume VII of *Tristram Shandy* and the *Journey* responded to this tradition in both a critically parodic and appreciative manner. There is a long list of authors who would have inspired Sterne, but Curley nevertheless concludes that "[w]hatever its debt to humanistic and scientific conventions of travel, *A Sentimental Journey* is, finally, a radically innovative travelogue, imbued with a bracing emotional and imaginative response to human life that authors of the Romantic Age would make famous". According to Curley, the break with tradition lies in Sterne's "subjective approach and exclusive attention to unlocking the inner sanctum of the human psyche by means of his sympathetic imagination and feeling", which is achieved in "a breathless Shandean style".[11]

Curley's approach is illustrative of the two critical *topoi* in travel writing studies that I would like to address and problematise in this chapter –

Sterne's agency in the so-called paradigm shift from the scientific to the subjective in travel writing and the vague concept of "Sternean/Shandean fashions", which has tended to be used as an umbrella term for stylistic idiosyncrasies in post-1768 travel writing. I will approach the former as reflective of a "mythical" style of reception that yearns to establish a myth of origin. The latter will be analysed with reference to the East Central European notion of *sternizm*, and will exemplify a pattern of disconnection, where a critical term derived from a name begins an autonomous life of its own and loses contact with the point of origin.

In tackling the first critical *topos*, I would like to begin by asking: was *A Sentimental Journey* the first "subjective" or "sentimental" travel account, exposing qualities that would become typical of Romantic travel writing? Was Sterne the solitary agent in the paradigm shift of the travel narrative as a genre?

In travel writing studies Sterne's *Journey* is typically treated as a prototype of the sentimental travel account, breaking with the tradition of the "scientific" or "impersonal" travelogue and undermining the institution of the Grand Tour. For example, Magdalena Dąbrowska contextualises her discussion of the Russian sentimental travelogue: "It was then [the turn of the eighteenth century] that the genre of sentimental travel developed in Russia. The genre was initiated in 1768 by Laurence Sterne".[12] Similar statements appear in C.W. Thompson's *French Romantic Travel Writing*, where we read about Sterne's giving "the radically self-conscious and subjective turn ... to sentimental travel".[13] Izabela Kalinowska, in turn, approaching Adam Mickiewicz's "Crimean Sonnets" as a travelogue, introduces Sterne as a background against which the tradition of Romantic travel of "internal landscapes" developed. Sterne is mentioned here as the one who rebelled against Grand Tour conventions and as such "marked a turning point in the history of travel writing as a genre".[14] At times, travel writing scholars appear to be more cautious and avoid definitive statements, even if the implication remains that it was Sterne's *Journey* that triggered the paradigm shift. For example, Carl Thompson devotes a whole section to what he terms the "inward turn" in travel writing and emphasises the role of Sterne. He refrains from labelling him the "first" and goes for the phrasing "an important early model" – not that there are any other early models mentioned in this respect.[15] As one would expect, when Sterne's contribution is discussed, Thompson yields to the temptation and avails himself of conventional vocabulary, for example by writing that *A Sentimental Journey* "introduced techniques for the representation of the self".[16]

When *A Sentimental Journey* is treated as the first of a kind, the new genre tends to be defined with Yorick's words: "'tis a quiet journey of the heart in pursuit of Nature, and those affections which rise out of her, which make us love each other—and the world, better than we do".[17] The idea that a genre can be "initiated" with the publication of a single text is itself a bold statement, but I would like to ponder further Yorick's definition in the context of eighteenth-century *ars apodemica*, or the art of travel.

Two years before the publication of *A Sentimental Journey*, Sterne elaborates upon travelling in the sermon "The Prodigal Son" published in the third volume of *Sermons of Mr. Yorick* (1766). On the one hand, his remarks are clearly grounded in the discourse on the merits of travel in the context of the Grand Tour. Like a number of his predecessors, such as Richard Lassels in *The Voyage of Italy* (1670) or John Locke in *Some Thoughts Concerning Education* (1693), Sterne enumerates the advantages of travel (if we "order it rightly"):

> ——to learn the languages, the laws and customs, and understand the government and interest of other nations,——to acquire an urbanity and confidence of behaviour, and fit the mind more easily for conversation and discourse;——to take us out of the company of our aunts and grandmothers, and from the track of nursery mistakes; and by shewing us new objects, or old ones in new lights, to reform our judgements——[18]

Then, in a manner that foreshadows the definition in *A Sentimental Journey*, Sterne turns to focus on human nature. Having defined man's natural disposition towards mobility – "The love of variety, or curiosity of seeing new things ... seems wove into the frame of every son and daughter of Adam" – he gets to his main point:

> ——by tasting perpetually the varieties of nature, to know what is good——by observing the address and arts of men, to conceive what is sincere,——and by seeing the difference of so many various humours and manners,——to look into ourselves and form our own.[19]

Sterne highlights the possibility not only to unravel the mysteries of human nature but also to develop a deeper understanding of personal identity, in a way paraphrasing Michel de Montaigne's metaphor that the world is "the mirror in which we must look in order to recognize ourselves from the proper angle".[20] Seen in this light, Yorick's definition of sentimental journeying does not radically break with the tradition of eighteenth-century travel. Defining the aim as the study of nature rather than objects of tourist interest does nevertheless highlight the educational value of travel. When the definition is used as a marker of the paradigm shift in travel writing, it is reflective of a critical misconception that is based on a one-sided reading of the definition. Its meaning is reduced to a sentimental slogan: a kind of "love others and know then thyself". This reading ignores the double-voiced poetics of the journey, the ambiguities peppering the narrative and the frivolous remarks throughout. It is enough to pair the definition with the other formulation of Yorick's aims – "But I could wish ... to spy the *nakedness* of their [i.e. the French women's] hearts"[21] – to see the perils of taking Yorick's sensibility for granted. It is worth highlighting that this statement is followed by a criticism of conventional Grand Tour objects of interests and then by the "pursuit of Nature" definition. Yorick openly ignores the Palais Royal or the Louvre, but what he chooses to concentrate on instead transcends straightforward sentimentalism. When such critical preconceptions determine the reading of Sterne's *Journey*, the effect invariably distorts what constitutes the text's reality.

For example, contrasting the *Journey* with *Tristram Shandy* with the intention of presenting the former as the prototype for the sentimental travel account, Dąbrowska maintains that Sterne shuns lengthy digressions and abandons his innovative typography, which clearly is not the case.[22] Such readings of the *Journey* are a belated manifestation of the policy of "sanitization" or "homogenization", to invoke Daniel Cook's and M-C. Newbould's respective labels for the strategies of sentimental anthologies at the turn of the eighteenth century.[23] The idea, as already mentioned in Chapter 2, was to ignore the complexity of the *Journey* and frame it into purely sentimental poetics.

To illustrate the weakness of the claim that Sterne alone paved the way for the "subjective" rather than "scientific" travelogue by radically breaking with the tradition of eighteenth-century travel, in particular the Grand Tour, I would like to refer to two travel texts that have been often contrasted with *A Sentimental Journey* – Tobias Smollett's *Travels through France and Italy* (1766) and Samuel Sharp's *Letters from Italy* (1767). The texts can be considered as the immediate context for the *Journey* both by virtue of publication date and because of the fact that they were identified by Sterne's Yorick himself, who invented satirical nicknames for their authors: the "learned Smelfungus" for the former, and "Mundungus" for the latter (though this identification may raise doubts).[24]

Excessive subjectivity, often credited to Sterne, is a dominant feature of Smollett's *Travels through France and Italy*. Smollett does not shun personalised remarks; indeed, he promotes his highly individualised perspective. This is tellingly foregrounded when he confronts recollections of his previous travels in France with the disappointing or sobering factuality of the here and now:

> Every object seems to have shrunk in its dimensions since I was
> last in Paris. The Louvre, the Palais-Royal, the bridges, and the
> river Seine, by no means answer the ideas I had formed of them
> from my former observation. When the memory is not very cor-
> rect, the imagination always betrays her into such extravagances.[25]

Drawing attention to the changing perspective of the focaliser, Smollett
undermines the conventional representational agenda of Grand Tour
travel accounts: that is, to offer factual information for those preparing
for their own ventures abroad, and to provide reliable resource for gaining
second-hand experience for armchair travellers. Smollett's idiosyncrasies
in terms of objects of interest, meanwhile, become a logical consequence
of this individualised perspective. One good example is his apparent
obsession with bridges; indeed, in a truly Shandean (if not Uncle Tobean)
manner, Smollett mentions or describes in greater detail about three
dozen bridges in his account. Among them is one of the bridges in Lyon:

> The bridge over the Rhone seems to be so slightly built, that I should
> imagine it would be one day carried away by that rapid river; especially
> as the arches are so small, that, after great rains they are sometimes
> *bouchées*, or stopped up; that is, they do not admit a sufficient passage
> for the encreased body of the water. In order to remedy this dangerous
> defect, in some measure, they found an artist some years ago, who has
> removed a middle pier, and thrown two arches into one. This alteration
> they looked upon as a masterpiece in architecture, though there is
> many a common mason in England, who would have undertaken and
> performed the work, without valuing himself much upon the enter-
> prize. This bridge ... is built, not in a strait line across the river, but
> with a curve, which forms a convexity to oppose the current. Such a
> bend is certainly calculated for the better resisting the general impetu-
> osity of the stream, and has no bad effect to the eye.[26]

Smollett's blend of factual knowledge and aesthetic issues, couched in a
style that juxtaposes straightforward simplicity ("no bad effect to the
eye") with convoluted syntax (especially at the beginning), as exempli-
fied by this passage, adds to the idiosyncratic poetics of *Travels*. The
traveller's appreciation of a curve rather than a straight line may thus
be taken as a metaphorically Shandean gesture, suggesting a departure
from the tradition of linear and factual travel narratives.

Smollett's departure from "scientific" travel writings also reveals
itself in his non-standard responses to tourist and artistic highlights, a
quality recognised by Sterne's Yorick himself in the well-known

comment on the "learned Smelfungus", who could not appreciate the value of the Pantheon or the Venus of Medicis. Writing about this singular take on the arts, William Gibson insightfully argues that the traveller's observations become "a form of iconoclasm" that allow him to make subjective remarks disconnected from the tradition of art appreciation and connoisseurship.[27] In this, Smollett turns out to be a proponent of sensibility, prioritising authentic responses of the observing subject, such as when he evaluates Guido Reni higher than Michelangelo,[28] or praises the true simplicity of the English garden.[29] He can dismiss renowned collections, labelling them a "magazine of painting",[30] and then elaborate on non-standard details, such as draperies, which he associates with artificiality: "nothing can be more monstrous, inconvenient, and contemptible, than the fashion of modern drapery".[31]

Smollett's spleen, earning him the title of "Splenetic Traveller" as distinguished by Mr. Yorick,[32] may be criticised in Sterne's *Journey*, but it is reflective of the same "inward turn" that some travel writing scholars credit exclusively to Sterne. Grzegorz Moroz correctly argues that the label "sentimental travel book" may well apply to Smollett's *Travels* despite the largely anti-sentimental travelling persona. What is more, following Casey Blanton's definition of the sentimental travel book as one that "foregrounds the narrator in an attempt to sentimentalize and/or glorify the narrator's experience in hostile environments", Moroz searches for proto-sentimental travel texts from the late sixteenth and seventeenth centuries.[33] This might take us a little too far, but the underlying assumption is apt: the "inward turn" was a far-reaching phenomenon, certainly beyond Sterne's contribution.

If Smollett's account exemplifies a self-centred travelogue predating *A Sentimental Journey*, Samuel Sharp's *Letters from Italy* is more a work of transition, where a typical Grand Tour narrative is interspersed with passages implying a weariness with its conventions. In the opening letter, Sharp promises to depart from the representational policy of the traditional Grand Tour account in a manner foreshadowing Sterne's vindication of interpersonal encounter over typical objects of interest. This is made clear in Letter 1:

> I do not mean to trouble you, or my other Friends during my stay abroad, with descriptions of statues, churches, and pictures; for, besides, that I can say no more on that subject than what every account of *Italy*, every guide for travellers, furnishes in a most tedious abundance, I have generally found the reading of such descriptions insipid and tiresome.[34]

Accordingly, there is no passage devoted to the crossing of the Alps, but only a mention of the route – by way of Geneva – which was chosen by Sharp so that he could pay a visit to Voltaire. The description of the meeting is rather loosely organised, and mostly involves a digression about Shakespeare's language and Voltaire's inability to sense it properly.

Even if the following letters offer perfectly conventional descriptive writing on the beauties and pleasures of Italy, and the manners of the Italians, complemented with factual information on boat travel, inns and other topics, this monotony is nevertheless disrupted by such curiosities as a "proto-Shandean" typographical embellishment representing the waving line of Canale Grande (see Figure 5.1),[35] a passage on "damp shirts" and "damp sheets",[36] or a detailed technological description of the operations of a mill alongside a drawing.[37]

That being said, attempts at undermining or even ridiculing the "scientific" travelogue were not first made by Sterne or his immediate predecessors. When on his Grand Tour, sometime around 1740, Horace Walpole wrote a *jeu d'esprit* "Walpole in Rome", which is a humorously chaotic catalogue-like account of the highlights Walpole decided not to see:

> **** Having heard that the best view of the city was from the top of St Peter's, which, as everyone knows, is not only the highest church in Rome, but in the world; for the tower of Babel, which as Sigonius supposes was a temple, is no longer standing; and the tower of Pequin, being an idolatrous place of worship, cannot properly be called a Christian church; I having a great desire to see at one prospect this mistress of the world —did not go up.[38]

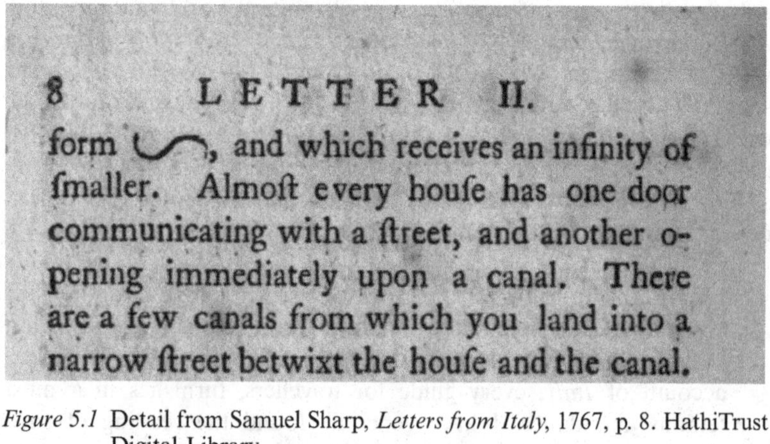
8 LETTER II.

form ~, and which receives an infinity of ſmaller. Almoſt every houſe has one door communicating with a ſtreet, and another o-pening immediately upon a canal. There are a few canals from which you land into a narrow ſtreet betwixt the houſe and the canal.

Figure 5.1 Detail from Samuel Sharp, *Letters from Italy*, 1767, p. 8. HathiTrust Digital Library.

Had this text been written three decades later, would it not have been considered as couched in a "Shandean style"? A passage like this one makes us ponder some more general questions about eponymous qualifiers of literary styles. What makes a style "Shandean"? How much Sterne is necessary for a style to be labelled "Sternean"? Needless to say, I am not trying to argue that Walpole's literary prank would have been a model for Sterne – it would have been highly unlikely for a piece first published in the twentieth century. However, what this passage and the rest following in the same vein testify to is the fact that, more than two decades before the publication of Volume VII of *Tristram Shandy* and *A Sentimental Journey*, Walpole's playful prank expressed a conviction that the genre and its conventions had become, as it were, exhausted.

To conclude this section, I would like to refer to a more balanced (and better-informed) approach to the "paradigm shift" offered by Barbara Korte. Having characterised Yorick's account in a rather conventional manner, she aptly concludes that *A Sentimental Journey* "consolidates tendencies which were also emerging in the travelogue proper and which became an increasingly important generic feature towards the end of the eighteenth century";[39] in particular, she sees the *Journey* as testimony to the gradual "increase in subjectivity" in contemporaneous travel writing.[40] She recognises Sterne's influence on thus directed development of the genre, but is far from crediting him with the title of father or originator. I share Korte's opinion, and the wording "consolidates" and "testimony" is a much more accurate recognition of Sterne's role.

As was hinted earlier, to a large extent Sterne's presence in historical and genealogical contexts in travel writing studies is a belated manifestation of late eighteenth-century trends in reception that created a Sterne who never was. As Peter de Voogd has recently written, "sentimental imitations rather than *A Sentimental Journey* itself created a curious vogue all over Europe ... and thus a Sterne who never existed".[41] The numerous editions of *The Beauties* as well as a plethora of sentimental imitations codified an understanding of Sterne that turned out to be a useful critical concept, especially for the study of the Romantic travelogue seen as a culmination of the subjective and fragmented tendencies in the life of the genre.

This leads me to the second aspect of Sterne's legacy in travel writing studies that I wish to ponder: the category of *sternizm*, which I briefly discussed in Chapter 4 as an umbrella term used in East Central European literary studies for narrative and stylistic idiosyncrasies in literature from the late eighteenth century onwards. The coinage itself is not exceptional – in Polish criticism it finds equivalents in *byronizm, ossianizm, youngizm* or *walterskotyzm*. The term itself is based upon a paradox,

which is noted by Kazimierz Bartoszyński, the author of an encyclopae-
dia entry that foregrounds *sternizm* as a significant phenomenon in Polish
Enlightenment and Romanticism. Bartoszyński is right to distinguish
between *sternizm* and Sterne's own characteristic features, drawing attention to the fact that the tendencies known as *sternizm* lived a life of their
own, often disconnected from Sterne himself.[42] In other words, there is
Sterne and his works, on the one hand, and a phenomenon that takes its
name after Sterne but need not be directly linked to the author, on the
other. As before, it again boils down to reception.

Even if Sterne's impact on a particular author was indeed the case
(as documented by explicit references and paratextual material, such as
correspondence [as discussed in Chapter 4]), conventional critical
commentary petrifies an understanding of Sterne's poetics that fails to
do justice to its complexity. For example, Maria Wirtemberska was
clearly an admirer of *A Sentimental Journey* and repetitiously made
clear the point of reference for her own literary ventures. However, the
following assessment of Wirtemberska's *sternizm* does little to link her
to Sterne convincingly:

> Like Sterne, Wirtemberska preserves an arrangement of chapters that
> corresponds to reality. She analogically constructs the main char-
> acter, who connects an account of the journey with detailed impres-
> sions and judgments. In a manner similar to the author of *A
> Sentimental Journey*, she frequently resorts to the technique of a
> detailed representation of scenes and people encountered. The choice
> of the objects of presentation reveals individual preferences.[43]

Dissecting the above, we end up with the following features of *sternizm*: subsequent chapters referring to the places visited, a narrative of
impressions and judgements, and a non-conventional choice of scenes
and people encountered described in detail. As this list makes clear, the
only quality that might indeed relate to *A Sentimental Journey* is non-
standard focus, though, as pointed out before with reference to Smollett and Sharp, this was not an exclusively Sternean feature.

Such a disconnection tends to result in abuses or appropriations of
Sterne and his method, and his alleged influence on texts or passages
whose authors would not have thought of Sterne at all. To give but one
example, Łucja Rautenstrauchowa's *In and Beyond the Alps* from 1840
has been read as an overtly sentimental travel account (which may well
be the case), clearly reflective of the Sternean fashions in Poland
(which raises doubts). To illustrate the disconnection between Sterne
himself and *sternizm*, I would like to quote two passages that have been

considered Sternean. The first is meant to exemplify "Sternean ... focus on solitary reflection":

> Little birds have already finished their evensong and were asleep in the bushes. Only in places did timid little stars glide their light along granite rocks through this dark night, or somewhere in the valley, one could see through the thick glass the little subdued lights of some poor household. ... Half asleep in the darkest corner of the carriage, I was musing about the Alps and about my Italian tour, for which I was making thousands and thousands of plans.[44]

The second, in which the traveller sympathises with a poor stranger, is labelled "pure imitation of Sterne":

> Oh, do cry, thought I deep in my soul, do cry, poor you, with all the tears of your heart; you, who are at daybreak buried under black clouds which will not let you bask in parental sunshine! You, who are embarking on life along a thorny path; when your peers enjoy their mothers' caresses and smiles, only cold selfishness, perhaps pride or contempt, await you in this world ... Lucky will you be to arouse pity! ... Oh, what terrible misery it is to call a stranger's *pity* your *luck*![45]

The passages may well be labelled sentimental, and thus illustrative of belated, clichéd sentimentality. But why does conventionalised sentimentalism prompt one to invoke the name of Sterne? If a poorly written account full of tears, solitary musings and emotional exclamations is enough to make us read a given passage as an example of *sternizm*, then we must realise the distance separating the work of Sterne and the "ism" coined after his name, or, more appropriately, the name of "Sterne who never existed", to repeat Peter de Voogd's apt remark.

Just as conventionalised sentimentality has been identified with "Sternean fashions", the figure of the sentimental traveller has been gradually deprived of the complexity with which Sterne endowed his Yorick. As I have argued elsewhere, Sterne's Yorick was a polyphonic character, oscillating between real life and fiction, sensibility and bawdiness, authenticity and playful irony.[46] Yorick's name has been frequently invoked with reference to Maria Wirtemberska's Malvina, who appears in *Malwina czyli Domyślność Serca* (1816; the English translation – *Malvina, or, The Heart's Intuition* – was published in 2001) and *Niektóre zdarzenia, myśli i uczucia doznane za granicą* (1816–1816). Indeed, Wirtemberska mentions Yorick's name herself, in a scene of alms-giving (Chapter XIV) clearly modelled on Sterne's analogical episode. That said, there is little in Wir-temberska's narrative that would corroborate the identification of Mal-vina with Yorick, all too often taken for granted. Alina Aleksandrowicz-Ulrich, a perceptive reader of Wirtemberska's work, underlined the limits of a "Sternean" reading of Malvina already in 1968. As she put it, "[Malvina] embodies a different type of sentimental traveller than Sterne's Yorick. She is indeed characterized by varying emotional states, but she lacks Yorick's complexity and ambiguity".[47]

I have not been trying to argue for Sterne's derivativeness and lack of ori-ginality, nor questioning his undeniable impact on English and Continental travel writing, especially in the final decades of the eighteenth century. As a matter of fact, by raising doubts about the two critical *topoi*, I aim to draw attention to the inherent limits of some of the popular binaries in literary criticism: convention versus innovation, originality versus derivativeness, novelty versus tradition. These tropes permeate critical discourse with a considerable frequency, but, more often than not, they tell much more about the critical standpoint than the discussed texts themselves. Sterne's afterlife, especially his presence in travel writing studies, makes for particularly strong evidence showing that these binaries distort rather than elucidate literary history. I have attempted to shed more light on this by discussing the limits of *sternizm* as a critical concept. *Sternizm*, when used without due attention devoted to Sterne himself, becomes a vague synonym for sentimentalism or Romantic irony; a qualifier highlighting a certain set of features distin-guishing a given travelogue from the early eighteenth-century tradition. Sterne and his work need not be an essential part of this.

Notes

This is an updated and developed version of the following article: "Sterne/ Yorick, the sentimental traveller and contemporary travel writing studies: problematising the critical afterlife of *A Sentimental Journey*". *Porównania* 24 (2019): 227–238.

1 "[T]his Species of writing … I have affirmed to be hitherto unattempted in our Language". Henry Fielding, *The History and Adventures of Joseph Andrews*, ed. Martin C. Battestin (Middletown, CT: Wesleyan University Press, 1967), 10.
2 Horace Walpole, *The Castle of Otranto*, ed. Nick Groom (Oxford: Oxford University Press, 2014), 13.
3 Having mentioned Rousseau, Johnson, Marivaux, Fielding, Richardson and Smollett as her noble predecessors, Burney writes: "I yet presume not to attempt pursuing the same ground which they have tracked". Frances Burney, *Evelina*, ed. Edward A. Bloom, intr. and notes Vivien Jones (Oxford: Oxford University Press, 2008), 10.

4 Laurence Sterne, *A Sentimental Journey and Continuation of the Bramine's Journal*, ed. Melvyn New and W. G. Day (Gainesville, FL: University Press of Florida, 2002), 15.
5 Laurence Sterne, *The Letters*, ed. Melvyn New and Peter de Voogd (Gainesville, FL: University Press of Florida, 2009), 536 (Feb. 23, 1767).
6 Thomas Keymer, *Sterne, the Moderns, and the Novel* (Oxford: Oxford University Press, 2002), 58.
7 Christopher Fanning, "Small Particles of Eloquence: Sterne and the Scriblerian Text", *Modern Philology* 100.3 (2003): 360–392.
8 Tim Parnell, "*The Sermons of Mr. Yorick*: The Commonplace and the Rhetoric of the Heart", in *The Cambridge Companion to Laurence Sterne*, ed. Thomas Keymer (Cambridge: Cambridge University Press, 2009), 76.
9 Thomas M. Curley, "Sterne's *A Sentimental Journey* and the Tradition of Travel Literature", in *All Before Them*, 1660–1780, ed. John McVeagh (London and Atlantic Highlands, NJ: The Ashfield Press, 1990), 203–216.
10 Curley, "Sterne's *A Sentimental Journey*", 203.
11 Curley, "Sterne's *A Sentimental Journey*", 213.
12 Magdalena Dąbrowska, "W stronę instrukcji. Listy z Londynu Piotra Makarowa w kontekście dyskusji nad gatunkiem podróży sentymentalnej w czasopismach rosyjskich początku XIX wieku" [Towards instruction: Peter Makarov's Letters from London and the debate on the genre of sentimental journey in Russian journals at the beginning of the nineteenth century], in *Metamorfozy podróży: Kultura i tożsamość* [Metamorphoses of the journey: Culture and Identity], ed. Jolanta Sztachelska et al. (Białystok: Wydawnictwo Uniwersytetu w Białymstoku, 2012), 65; trans. mine.
13 C.W. Thompson, *French Romantic Travel Writing: Chateaubriand to Nerval* (Oxford: Oxford University Press, 2012), 13.
14 Izabela Kalinowska, *Between East and West: Polish and Russian Nineteenth-Century Travel to the Orient* (Rochester, NY: University of Rochester Press, 2004), 24.
15 Carl Thompson, *Travel Writing* (London and New York: Routledge, 2011), 111.
16 Carl Thompson, *Travel Writing*, 112.
17 Sterne, *A Sentimental Journey*, 111.
18 Laurence Sterne, *The Sermons of Laurence Sterne*, ed. Melvyn New (Gainesville, FL: University Press of Florida, 1996), 192.
19 Sterne, *The Sermons*, 192.
20 Michel de Montaigne, *The Complete Essays of Montaigne* (Stanford, CA: Stanford University Press, 1958), 116.
21 Sterne, *A Sentimental Journey*, 111.
22 Magdalena Dąbrowska, *Dla pożytku i przyjemności: Rosyjska podróż sentymentalna przełomu XVIII i XIX wieku* [Useful pleasures: The Russian sentimental journey at the turn of the eighteenth century] (Warszawa: Wydawnictwa Uniwersytetu Warszawskiego, 2009), 51.
23 Daniel Cook, "Authors Unformed: Reading 'Beauties' in the Eighteenth Century", *Philological Quarterly* 89.2–3 (2010): 290; M-C. Newbould, "Wit and Humour for the Heart of Sensibility: The Beauties of Fielding and Sterne", in *The Afterlives of Eighteenth-Century Fiction*, ed. Daniel Cook and Nicholas Seager (Cambridge: Cambridge University Press, 2015), 136.
24 See Sterne, *A Sentimental Journey*, 272 (note 37.24).

25 Tobias Smollett, *Travels through France and Italy*, foreword by Ted Jones, intr. by Thomas Seccombe (New York: Tauris Parke, 2010), 93.
26 Smollett, *Travels through France and Italy*, 115.
27 William L. Gibson, *Art and Money in the Writings of Tobias Smollett* (Lewisburg: Bucknell University Press, 2007), 14; 109–136.
28 Smollett, *Travels through France and Italy*, 264.
29 Smollett, *Travels through France and Italy*, 262.
30 Smollett, *Travels through France and Italy*, 93.
31 Smollett, *Travels through France and Italy*, 99.
32 Sterne, *A Sentimental Journey*, 15.
33 Grzegorz Moroz, *Travellers, Novelists and Gentlemen: Constructing Male Narrative Personae in British Travel Books, from the Beginnings to the Second World War* (Frankfurt am Main: Peter Lang, 2013), 95; Casey Blanton, *Travel Writing: The Self and the World* (London and New York: Routledge, 2002), 13.
34 Samuel Sharp, *Letters from Italy* (London: Printed for R. Cave, 1767), 1–2.
35 Sharp, *Letters from Italy*, 8.
36 Sharp, *Letters from Italy*, 17.
37 Sharp, *Letters from Italy*, 272–273.
38 Horace Walpole, "Walpole in Rome", *The Yale Edition of Horace Walpole's Correspondence*, vol. 14, ed. W. S. Lewis (New Haven, CT: Yale University Press, 1948), 239.
39 Barbara Korte, *English Travel Writing: From Pilgrimages to Postcolonial Explorations*, trans. Catherine Matthias (London: Macmillan, 2000), 57.
40 Korte, *English Travel Writing*, 56.
41 Peter de Voogd, "Laurence Sterne and the 'Gutter of Time'", in *Studies in English Literature and Culture: Festschrift in Honour of Professor Grażyna Bystydzieńska*, ed. Anna Kędra-Kardela, Aleksandra Kędzierska, Magdalena Pypeć (Lublin: Maria Curie-Skłodowska University Press, 2017), 276. See also M-C. Newbould, *Adaptations of Laurence Sterne's Fiction: Sterneana, 1760–1840* (Burlington and Aldershot: Ashgate, 2013), esp. Chapter 2: "Sentimental Journeys?: Adaptations of Sterne's Travel Narratives".
42 Kazimierz Bartoszyński, "Sternizm", in *Słownik literatury polskiego oświecenia* [A dictionary of Polish Enlightenment literature], ed. Teresa Kostkiewiczowa (Wrocław: Ossolineum, 2002), 581.
43 Beata Kurządkowska, "Między rzeczywistością a fikcją w relacji z podróży Marii Wirtemberskiej 'Niektóre zdarzenia, myśli i uczucia doznane za granicą'" [Between reality and fiction in Maria Wirtemberska's travel account "Some occurrences, thoughts and emotions experienced abroad"], *Prace Literaturoznawcze* 1 (2013): 43; trans. mine.
44 Magdalena Ożarska, *Two Women Writers and their Italian Tours: Mary Shelley's Rambles in Germany and Italy and Łucja Rautenstrauchowa's In and Beyond the Alps* (Lewiston, NY: The Edwin Mellen Press, 2013), 62–63.
45 Ożarska, *Two Women Writers and their Italian Tours*, 64.
46 Jakub Lipski, *In Quest of the Self: Masquerade and Travel in the Eighteenth-Century Novel. Fielding, Smollett, Sterne* (Amsterdam and New York: Rodopi, 2014), 185–198.
47 Alina Aleksandrowicz-Ulrich, "Nieznana 'podróż' sentymentalna Marii Wirtemberskiej" [Maria Wirtemberska's unknown sentimental "journey"], *Pamiętnik Literacki* 59.2 (1968): 16.

6 Coda

The Eighteenth-Century Novel in the Age of Trump: Critical Revisions and Popular Appropriations

Why read, or indeed re-read, the eighteenth-century novel today? The five case studies in this book have demonstrated diverse ways in which *Robinson Crusoe, Tom Jones, Tristram Shandy* and *A Sentimental Journey* have inspired the following generations of writers, artists and critics, both transforming their material and uncovering new meanings in it. However vibrant these afterlives may be, or may have been, the key to the collective popular imagination in the twenty-first century lies elsewhere: in the socio-political potential of eighteenth-century fiction; in its adaptability to the topical concerns of the here and now. One observable characteristic of contemporary criticism and theory – and this by all means holds for eighteenth-century studies – is its activist agenda. Evan Gottlieb, an eighteenth-century studies scholar with a strong interest in theory, has recently written that:

> contemporary theory is distinguished by its interest in speculating on how we might move toward the creation of new, more egalitarian socio-political formations. ... I find it useful to think of contemporary theory in terms of its commitment to imagining new forms of individual and collective being and doing.[1]

These apt observations capture the essence of what might be labelled the socio-political turn in literary studies – a departure from text-oriented forms of criticism in quest of relevance and translatability of the literary into the social and political realities of the present. This often results in a separation of the literary work from its textual reality, which, in a sense, realises Jauss's wish to see literary works liberated from "the material of the words".[2] One good illustration of this would be the uses of the iconography of Margaret Atwood's *The Handmaid's Tale* (1985) in the context of feminist protests.[3] Such a liberation from the literary can, of course, be prompted by cinematic or television afterlives, as was

DOI: 10.4324/9781003153016-10

undoubtedly the case for *The Handmaid's Tale* and its internationally acclaimed TV adaptation (Hulu, 2017–). But visual afterlives alone, however popular, are not the decisive factor: it would be risky to assume that all those who don the handmaid's costume as a form of protest have actually seen the series, not to mention read the book. One should not ignore the intra-textual socio-political agenda, either – the turn towards activism in artistic practices is nothing new under the sun. Be that as it may, the implied patterns of reception in the twenty-first century, both for the critic and the mythical "average reader", are rarely confined to the realm of the literary, and instead tend to nod towards the realities of their social context.

Two eighteenth-century texts stand out as having undoubtedly succeeded in making a name for themselves beyond the circles of their actual readership; that is, they have long been universally recognised as adaptable works, and have thus provided material endlessly subject to appropriation even by those who might not have taken the trouble to read them. These two texts are Daniel Defoe's *Robinson Crusoe* and Jonathan Swift's *Gulliver's Travels* – everybody "knows" these narratives, even if comparatively few have actually read them (in their entirety). "Knowing" *Crusoe* and *Gulliver* is part of cultural competence, very much like "knowing" Hamlet's "to be or not to be", Dracula's teeth, Frankenstein's "monster" (though here the difficulty may lie in realising that the creature's name is not Frankenstein), or indeed the handmaid's costume. The reasons for the status of Defoe's and Swift's stories are manifold, and their presence in the collective popular imagination is an outcome of such factors as mythical and archetypal dimensions, continuous trans-medial adaptability, and a combination of universalist anthropological insights and socio-political relevance at different historical moments. In what follows, I will discuss some of the most recent appropriations of *Crusoe* and *Gulliver* beyond the realm of literature, as well as evaluating the socio-political potential of other eighteenth-century novels, such as Samuel Richardson's *Pamela* and Olaudah Equiano's *Interesting Narrative*, in the context of the topical issues of a period labelled by some the Age of Trump (2016–2020): the 2016 Trump election, Brexit, the #MeToo movement and the recent Black Lives Matter protests.

The fascinating subject of "Trump and eighteenth-century fiction" has been explored in a variety of ways, from the fake Trump tweets evaluating literary classics, such as *Tristram Shandy* ("Halfway through this biography and the main character isn't even born yet. Bad writing and a very weak way to tell a story. Hard to read!"[4]) and a discussion of naked Trump statues (drawing attention to alleged sex scandals) as a type of "secret history". This genre was very popular in the long eighteenth century and seen as "integrally tied to citizen action – the act of refusing to remain passive and obedient, the act of claiming ownership of secrets in which one has an interest".[5] Meanwhile, Trump's inaugural address has been read with reference to the imperialist ideology of Augustan poetry and fiction.[6] That said, the uses of this curious relationship for the purposes of socio-political activism have become the most vivid in connection with Swift's *Gulliver's Travels* and its satirical potential.

Journalist Roderick Kefferpütz put forward the phrase "Gulliver strategy" as a way to hinder Trump's political moves, "a convergence of many different smaller actors to contain him", recalling the famous scene from Part I, where gigantic Gulliver is tied and immobilised by a hoard of Lilliputians.[7] In cultural terms, the "Gulliver strategy" may well include the political use of Swift's imagery to respond critically to Trump's policies. This contributes to the 350-year-long tradition of actualising Swiftian satire and adjusting it to the ever changing here and now,[8] a phenomenon that stems from a well-recognised quality of Swift's parody in *Gulliver's Travels*, which, in the words of Claude Rawson, "transcends its immediate object".[9] Indeed, as Laurence Keogh puts it, "there's a continual supply of targets out there that are just begging for a bit of Swiftian commentary",[10] Trump clearly being a favourite choice. The recent popular appropriators of the satirical message of *Gulliver's Travels* and its visual afterlives have placed the former president in such roles as Gulliver himself or the Emperor of Lilliput, as well as bringing in the recognisable features of the wider socio-political panorama of the Age of Trump, thus following in the footsteps of such giants of visual political satire as James Gillray, Isaac Cruickshank and Thomas Nast and their Swiftian prints (including Gillray's caricature of Napoleon and George III in "The King of Brobdingnag and Gulliver" from 1803 [Figure C.1], "one of the most reproduced and instantly recognizable political caricatures in British history", as David Taylor points out[11]). More recently, *Gulliver's Travels* has been adapted by *The Guardian*'s cartoonist and graphic novelist Martin Rowson, who is known for his interest in the eighteenth-century novel.[12]

Two recent artworks depicting Trump as Gulliver in Lilliput merit attention. The first one is a painting by Californian artist Olga Hofmann titled "Gulliver Trump in the divided land of Lillipublicans and Blefucrats" (2017), which, rather than implying any Trump-oriented political commentary, uses Swiftian satire to picture the wider spectrum of social and political divisions in post-2016 America, representing a fractured society and a cacophony of empty slogans, as well as touching upon the allegations of the Russian interference and the role of the media.[13] The other piece is a cartoon depicting the "Gulliver strategy" with reference to the roping scene,

Figure C.1 James Gillray, "The King of Brobdingnag and Gulliver", 1803. Metropolitan Museum of Art.

but here with a clearly Trumpist agenda. Ben Garrison's 2019 "The Giant Awakens" (Figure C.2) sees heroic Trump-Gulliver tearing the ropes to press the emergency button. This is meant to signal a call for another "Great Awakening", allowing society to see the true (here caricatured) faces of such crazy Lilliputians as "OCRAZYO CORTEZ", "OBAMA", "HILLARY" and – inevitably – "SOROS" hiding in the bushes of the swamp.

Figure C.2 Ben Garrison. "The Giant Awakens", 2019. © Ben Garrison. Courtesy of Ben Garrison.

This framing of Gulliver as a national hero, also present in Garrison's "The Sleeping Giant Finally Wakes Up" from 2013,[14] and the resulting reorientation of satire towards the Lilliputians, finds a notable, if comic, antecedent in William Hogarth's "The Punishment inflicted on Lemuel Gulliver" (1726). This image shows a hoard of caricatured Lilliputians who perform an enema on the protagonist as punishment for the well-known manner by which he extinguished the fire in the Empress of Lilliput's apartment. Ronald Paulson has interpreted the scene (which does not feature in Swift's narrative itself) as "an image of the honest Englishman ... who stupidly gives up his 'liberty' to these pygmy politicians and clergymen".[15]

The association between Trump's politics and Swift's narrative was in part triggered by the fact that 2017 was both the opening year of Trump's presidency and of the "Swift at 350" anniversary, which understandably directed critical energy towards the Irish satirist, as well as renewing general interest in the writer. This blend of research activities and popular appeal resulted both in new scholarly work on Swift with Trump as a point of reference (for example, in discussions of "post-truth" or "fake news",[16] somehow prophesised by the author of *Gulliver's Travels*) and politically engaged artwork, both supportive and critical. The ultimate bond between the eighteenth-century writer and America's 45th president, which Swift would no doubt have appreciated, was created when Trump appeared in Irish artist Hugh Madden's mural (Figure C.3), which ornamented Swift's birthplace to celebrate the 2017 anniversary: it features Trump as the Emperor of Lilliput represented in a manner reminiscent of Gillray's print.

Swift's work and views have also been invoked with reference to Brexit, for example by readers seeing parallels between some crucial aspects of the current debate and the Anglo-Irish relationship as commented upon in *The Drapier's Letters* (1724–1725),[17] or between the Anglo-Irish trade conflicts in Swift's day and the likely economic repercussions of a no-deal Brexit.[18] In a more straightforward manner, Brexit has been labelled "a Modest Proposal" or "a Swiftian solution", with the latter meant to refer to the former rather than Swift's own political standpoint.[19] A neo-Swiftian novel has even appeared: *Boy Giant: Son of Gulliver* by Michael Morpurgo (2019), which, as the author makes clear, was inspired by both Trump's politics and Brexit.[20] That said, the parallel that can arguably tell

Figure C.3 Hugh Madden, Detail from *Gulliver's Travels* Mural in Hoey Place, Dublin. 2017. Courtesy of Hugh Madden.

us more about the historical origins of Brexit as an idea is that which links the Leave vote with *Robinson Crusoe*.

Naval historian Andrew Lambert, in an attempt to justify the ways of Leave campaigners to men, used *Crusoe* as a paradigmatic text for understanding the specificity of British insular identity:

> Defoe's book helped shape the mental world of 18th century Britain. Today it reminds us that Britain is far more intimately connected with South Asia, the West Indies, Africa and the rest of the world beyond Europe than it is with the continent itself.

Crusoe's Island, he adds, is a "microcosm" that offers unique "insight into a distinctive English identity", constituted, hopefully among other things, by "a profound aversion to being told what to do by foreigners"[21] – an idea developed by Lambert in a book that elaborates on Crusoe's Island as a "mirror held up to the English".[22] The nostalgic feelings of a naval historian in this respect are perfectly understandable, but the suggestion that *Robinson Crusoe* reflects an essential "aversion of being told what to do by foreigners" should perhaps be complemented by the fact that it is English sailors whom Robinson pacifies by way of an intrigue with his friend the Spaniard towards the end of Volume 1. It is the English, too, who commit genocide in *Farther Adventures*, as a result of which Robinson wants to have nothing to do with them. Lambert also overlooks Defoe's ridicule of ethnic and national essentialism in "The True-Born Englishman" (1701).

A similarly one-sided view on *Robinson Crusoe* dominates Robert Clark's thorough and both scholarly and political discussion of "Robinsonade and Brexit", where he elaborates on the "imperial unconscious" as the common denominator of *Crusoe*, the Robinsonade, as well as the Leave campaign and Brexit discourse in general.[23] Clark persuasively argues that Crusoe's "desert" island should rather be viewed as "deserted", or cleansed, for that matter, and that the fantasies of uninhabited fertile islands repress the colonial truth about the exploitation and annihilation of native peoples. In fact, this truth, as mentioned above, is far from being repressed in the *Crusoe* trilogy, and Defoe's Robinson is much more than a narrow-minded coloniser. Apparently, what would have contributed to such an understanding of *Crusoe* is the rich tradition of the colonial Robinsonade, thriving in the Victorian period alongside the gradual spread and growth of the British Empire; this is mentioned by Clark but should perhaps constitute the core of the Robinson-Brexit parallel.[24] This is not to say that there are no colonial undertones in *Robinson Crusoe*, but to highlight the complexity of Defoe's novel and worldview, especially when compared with a number of rather straightforward castaway narratives in the nineteenth century, which, as Susan Maher put it, "recast their Crusoes into quintessential empire builders, create islands that signify a hierarchy of culture and race, and ultimately mirror a conquering people's mythology".[25] So, rather than placing Crusoe himself in the role of a proto-Brexiteer, it is perhaps more accurate to re-read the Robinsonade tradition in this context. Indeed, the vast corpus of satirical Brexit cartoons referring to the iconography of desert islands, instead of invoking Defoe's Robinson, tends to frame contemporary characters, anonymous and well-known, in more general castaway narrative patterns, such as shipwreck or solitude on an island, with the proactive ideologies of imperial narratives mocked by representations of inertia, solitude and emptiness.

Robinsonade iconography has been adopted with reference to Brexit by such prominent figures in the field of contemporary graphic satire as *The Guardian*'s Steve Bell ("European Raft"),[26] *Charlie Hebdo*'s Laurent Sourisseau ("Les Anglais enfin maîtres chez eux"),[27] *The Evening Standard*'s Christian Adams ("Together at Last" and "Unloved Island – The Contestants")[28] or the *Financial Times*'s Ingram Pinn ("Boris Johnson is wrong. Parliament has the ultimate authority").[29] The notable castaway figures included David Cameron, Theresa May, Jeremy Corbyn, Boris Johnson as well as the "average Briton". These are all hilarious and skilful cartoons, but one work demonstrates an understanding of the Robinsonade's metaphorical and metonymical dimensions that deserves closer attention. It is, in fact, the most recent one of the group, created after four years of national divisions and largely unsuccessful negotiations, which might explain a departure from caricature towards an iconography of straightforward and poignant simplicity. "Post-Brexit Britain" (Figure C.4) by Tjeerd Royaards, an award-wining Dutch cartoonist whose work has appeared in *The Guardian, Der Spiegel* and *Le Monde*, among others, develops the metonymical relationship between the island, the body and the mind, which has been explored in both Robinsonade criticism and fiction.[30]

Here the potentially caricatured face of Boris Johnson is largely invisible. It is covered almost completely by the well-known haircut, which blinds him and constitutes a barren island of unhappiness, where even the paradigmatic palm tree struggles to survive – an imperial fantasy of the Prime Minister's mind, the effects of which he cannot see. The islands of Robinsonades are typically fertile, presenting the castaway with an abundance of fauna and flora, manageable climate and various forms of shelter and sustenance. Johnson's island as depicted here offers none of these; instead, it becomes a locus of an anti-Robinsonade, very much like the waste land depicted in J.M. Coetzee's *Foe* (as discussed in Chapter 1).

Figure C.4 Tjeerd Royards, "Post-Brexit Britain". © Tjeerd Royaards, Cartoon Movement.

If the relevance of *Robinson Crusoe* and *Gulliver's Travels* in the Age of Trump stems from a centuries-long tradition of adapting and re-using these texts (which themselves, to paraphrase Claude Rawson's remark upon Swift's work, "transcend their immediate object"), the socio-political turmoil of the recent years has also resulted in other appropriations and actualisations of eighteenth-century fiction. In particular, the global protests under the labels of #MeToo and #BlackLivesMatter seem to have renewed interest in cultural representations of power structures and issues of gender and race more broadly, also in the field of eighteenth-century fiction. This has encouraged such forms of critical and cultural activism as research into so-called rape studies, #BlackLivesMatter exhibitions of art, MeToo and BLM reading lists or literary events for the public. The question is whether this socio-political context constitutes an opportunity for other eighteenth-century novels to become part of the collective popular imagination.

Chloe Wigston Smith in her *Conversation* article on "How harassed women had their #MeToo moments in the 18th century" sketches the possibilities for selected eighteenth-century texts to gain in topicality against this background; the "MeToo narratives" she foregrounds are Samuel Richardson's *Pamela; or, Virtue Rewarded* (1742) and Eliza Haywood's *Fantomina* (1725).[31] A crypto-appeal to the popular audience,

Smith's choice of Richardson's *Pamela* over *Clarissa* (1748), whose tragic mode would make it an even more adequate choice for the MeToo reading list, is arguably more than just a realist and reasonable solution given the size of the respective texts: the two volumes of *Pamela* stand a better chance with "the average reader" than the nine volumes of *Clarissa*. Inadvertently, perhaps, the foregrounding of Pamela as a MeToo victim engages with the so-called *Pamela* controversy in the mid-eighteenth century, that is, the critical and creatively interartistic responses to Richardson's original, provoked by the moral ambiguity of what we would now label "Pamela's MeToo". In brief, some eighteenth-century readers of Richardson's novel found Pamela's claim for virtue problematic, and instead focused on the "rewarded" part of the subtitle, and treated the narrative as a case of making a living, as well as securing one's social ascension, on what might be termed the capital of chastity. This kind of reading resulted in a vibrant reception of Richardson's novel, also parodic, with such notable counter-narratives as Henry Fielding's *Shamela* (1741) or Eliza Haywood's *The Anti-Pamela* (1741), both of which drew attention to the mercantilist handling of "virtue" on the heroine's part, and were among as many as "five significant 'counter-fictions'" that came out no longer than a year after *Pamela*'s publication.[32]

Current MeToo discourse, however, emphasises that such stories of "success" are, in fact, all the more representative of the wider power structures inherent in a culture of abuse, and that even a conceited and scheming Shamela, trading on her "vartue" (a very much telling blend of virtue and value), remains after all a victim of her social context. Seen in this light, the choice of Pamela over Clarissa as a potential icon of the MeToo movement is both a gesture towards resolving the "*Pamela* controversy" and a potentially strategic move based on the assumption that less straightforward examples work more forcibly, especially as *Clarissa*'s explicit engagement with the "culture of rape" might be too much for the modern reader to handle. Yoon Son Lee, a professor of English at Wellesley College, thus reflects on *Clarissa*'s disturbing content:

> I began teaching the abridged version in my "Rise of the Novel" class. For a time, I even dreamed of teaching an entire course on the novel. But after 2016, my feelings did a 180. I came to view it in a completely different light. I'm hardly able to read the letters from Lovelace, which make up a large part of the novel. Reading it after #MeToo, I'm not sure if I can teach it again.[33]

Pamela's subtler poetics, the narrative's more reasonable length, rich visual and textual afterlife, as well as the fact that its claim for the title of "first English novel" still finds followers,[34] all support its potential presence in the collective popular imagination. The vocabulary that journalist Rowan Pelling uses in her *Telegraph* article on *Pamela* and MeToo is suggestive of the kind of popularising language that could earn Richardson's novel this status. Clearly, *Pamela* does not have to be "rediscovered" in academic circles, so the titular "rediscovering of a 1740s blockbuster" creates an aura of sensationalism that is meant to enable a smooth transition into the realm of the popular.[35]

Pamela's potential role as an archetypal MeToo narrative in the wider terrain of culture and entertainment has not yet fully materialised. What it clearly needs is a vibrant audio-visual afterlife: whilst there has been a relatively well-received miniseries based on *Clarissa*, starring Sean Bean and Saskia Wickham (BBC, 1991), the sex comedy *Mistress Pamela* from 1973 was little more than a caricature of the possibilities offered by the novel. In this context, the critical and commercial success of the National Theatre's 2019 production *When We Have Sufficiently Tortured Each Other* with Cate Blanchett in the main role, is a promising sign showing how the novel can be powerfully actualised for a present-day audience. The play consists of 12 scenes directly alluding to *Pamela*, and the playwright, Martin Crimp, was especially interested in Richardson's "sense of enclosure",[36] that is, his handling of power structures in a closed, prison-like environment, which is easily translatable into various contexts, from academia to film industry, as the plethora of MeToo stories have revealed.[37]

Unlike the largely ahistorical, or universally panhistorical, MeToo movement, the Black Lives Matter protests throughout the Age of Trump, and more recently in the wake of the death of George Floyd, have invariably demonstrated a historical sensitivity in understanding contemporary institutionalised racism as a product of Western imperialism and the slave trade. Since both these phenomena flourished in the long eighteenth century, it is not surprising that the period's cultural content surfaces in BLM activism. The most vivid manifestation of this was the toppling of slave trader Edward Colston's (1636–1721) statue in Bristol, which prompted Jonathan Sacks to conclude that the eighteenth century is "more relevant than ever".[38]

This begs the question of the early novel's relevance in this context, and its potential adaptability to serve the BLM cause. As a rule, racial others in most of the eighteenth-century fictional corpus are not given a chance to go beyond their predetermined roles within the imperialist structures. Such works as Aphra Behn's *Oroonoko* (1688) or Defoe's *Crusoe* have indeed been invoked with reference to BLM, but understandably in no favourable light. Behn's representation of the royal slave, even if intended to raise awareness of the horrors of slavery, has been recognised as fully indebted to the colonial repertory of "deeply racist and dehumanising tropes".[39] Defoe, a shareholder in the Royal African Company and author of "racist" *Robinson Crusoe*, is unlikely to escape the scrutiny of the controversial "Plaque review", which is intended to verify the potentially disturbing content, or "problematic connotations", of English Heritage's blue plaques in London.[40]

If an eighteenth-century novel is ever to make it onto a BLM reading list, the most likely work would be the autobiographical *Interesting Narrative* by Olaudah Equiano from 1789, written and published in the context of the late eighteenth-century abolitionist movement as a piece of life writing, which, however, demonstrates a number of fictional strategies ranging from the picaresque to the Robinsonade.[41] With several scholarly editions published to date, the importance of Equiano's *Narrative* in the field of criticism is now taken for granted. Its pertinence in the light of the BLM protests has also been appreciated: the official BLM website offers a brief historical profile of Equiano, as well as providing a link to the BBC4 documentary "The Extraordinary Equiano" (2005),[42] while the Equiano Society is indomitable in promoting his life and work using predominantly public-facing platforms of dissemination, such as popular exhibitions and open events. The writer and his *Narrative* may deservedly benefit from the project to "reinvent" history,[43] but whether this will eventually translate into a wider popular recognition remains to be seen.

This book has been finalised in a time of lockdown and the Covid-19 pandemic. The first-hand experience of plague made me turn to its literary representations, such as Daniel Defoe's *A Journal of the Plague Year* (1722). I thought it was a hobby-horsical mannerism of an eighteenth-centuryist but was surprised to see that the few available second-hand copies of the Polish edition of Defoe's novel were on sale at roughly 500% of their pre-Covid prices. In the UK, *The Telegraph* reports, the novel had to be reprinted after selling out.[44] This is testament to how the eighteenth-century novel persistently resonates with the here and now, and the worldwide interest in the novel as recorded by Google Trends (Figure C.5) reveals a striking correspondence to the two respective epidemic waves.

Defoe's *Journal* is unlikely to enjoy an afterlife comparable to that of *Robinson Crusoe* or *Gulliver's Travels* but its swift transition into the popular, its foregrounded position in a number of recommended Covid reading lists,[45] shows that it is not unreasonable to assume that similar, even if short-lived, rediscoveries of eighteenth-century novels will take place in the context of topical socio-political issues in the years to

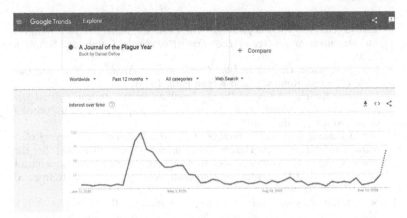

Figure C.5 Google Trends line graph of interest in Daniel Defoe's *Journal of the Plague Year* in 2020 worldwide.

come. Such popular revisions, often verging on political appropriation, need not answer to what eighteenth-century texts meant in their own contexts; they go beyond the "tyranny of the original"[46] by recognising its adaptability, topicality and continuous relevance, and, indeed, by showing that the eighteenth century has not finished.

Notes

1 Evan Gottlieb, *Engagements with Contemporary Literary and Critical Theory* (London and New York: Routledge, 2020), 4.

2 Hans Robert Jauss, *Toward an Aesthetic of Reception* (Minneapolis: University of Minnesota Press, 1982), 21.

3 "How The Handmaid's Tale Costumes in Protests Impact Political Change", *CBC News: The National* (You Tube, 7 June 2019), www.youtube.com/watch?v=bxPaX79U6RI.

4 This fake tweet, and similar ones, are no longer available. Robin Bates has commented on the puns in in Robin Bates, "If Trump Tweeted Classic Lit Reviews…", *Better Living through Beowulf* (16 March 2016), https://betterlivingthroughbeowulf.com/imagining-trump-as-a-lit-critic.

5 Alyssia Garrison, "Those Naked Donald Trump Statues? They Have a Secret History", *The National Book Review* (2 November 2016), https://www.thenationalbookreview.com/features/2016/11/2/essay-those-naked-donald-trump-statues-they-have-a-secret-history.

6 Spencer Jackson, *We Are Kings: Political Theology and the Making of a Modern Individual* (Charlottesville: University of Virginia Press, 2020), 1–2.

7 Roderick Kefferpütz, "Trumping Trump: A Gulliver Strategy", *Medium* (6 July 2017), https://medium.com/everyvote/trumping-trump-a-gulliver-strategy-3fc96e4d5d93.

8   See Jonathan McCreedy, Vesselin M. Budakov and Alexandra K. Glava-nakova (eds.), *Swiftian Inspirations: The Legacy of Jonathan Swift from the Enlightenment to the Age of Post-Truth* (Newcastle: Cambridge Scholars, 2020).

9   Claude Rawson, *Gulliver and the Gentle Reader: Studies in Swift and Our Time* (London: Routledge and Kegan Paul, 1973), 37.

10 Laurence Keogh, "A City of Words: Jonathan Swift", *Dublin: Official Site for News, Information and Events* (2017), https://dublin.ie/live/stories/city-of-words-jonathan-swift.

11 David Francis Taylor, *The Politics of Parody: A Literary History of Caricature, 1760–1830* (New Haven: Yale University Press, 2018), 181. See the whole Chapter 6, "Gulliver Goes to War", for an excellent discussion of Gillray's print in the context of eighteenth-century graphic satire inspired by *Gulliver's Travels*.

12 See Martin Rowson, *Gulliver's Travels* (London: Atlantic Books, 2012); Martin Rowson, *The Life and Opinions of Tristram Shandy* (London: Picador, 1996); and his illustrations to a recent edition of Laurence Sterne, *A Sentimental Journey*, ed. Patrick Wildgust and Helen Williams (Coxwold: Shandy Hall Press, 2018).

13 For a detailed commentary on the piece, see Vesselin M. Budakov, Jonathan McCreedy and Alexandra K. Glavanakova, "Introduction", in *Swiftian Inspirations*, xv-xvi. The picture is represented on the cover of their monograph.

14 Ben Garrison, "The Sleeping Giant Finally Wakes Up", https://grrrgraphics.com/sleeping-giant-finally-wakes-up.

15 Ronald Paulson, "Putting out the Fire in Her Imperial Majesty's Apartment: Opposition Politics, Anticlericalism, and Aesthetics", *ELH* 63.1 (1996): 82.

16 2016 saw "post-truth" declared the Oxford Word of the Year, while in 2017 Collins Dictionary credited "fake news" with the same title.

17 Jonathan McCreedy, "Is Brexit the Modern-Day 'Wood's Halfpence'? Re-Evaluating Swift's Economic Policies in a Time of Contemporary Crisis and Uncertainty in Ireland", in *Swiftian Inspirations*, 225–246.

18 Brendan Keenan, "View from Dublin: What Jonathan Swift Would Say about Brexit", *Belfast Telegraph* (16 April 2019), www.belfasttelegraph.co.uk/business/analysis/view-from-dublin-what-jonathan-swift-would-say-about-brexit-38014353.html.

19 See Michael Carlson, "Brexit: A Modest Proposal", *ARC* (8 October 2019), https://arcdigital.media/brexit-a-modest-proposal-124e47ec6c1e, and Paul Vallely, "Paul Vallely on Brexit and Ireland: A Swiftian Solution", *Church Times* (19 October 2018), www.churchtimes.co.uk/articles/2018/19-october/comment/columnists/paul-vallely-on-brexit-and-ireland-a-swiftian-solution.

20 Etan Smallman, An Interview with Michael Morpurgo: "Michael Morpurgo on Fighting Brexit: 'I've been spat at. It's almost civil war'", *The Guardian* (13 September 2019), www.theguardian.com/books/2019/sep/13/michael-morpurgo-boy-giant-brexit-refugee-crisis-trump-civil-war.

21 Andrew Lambert, "What Robinson Crusoe Can Teach Us about Brexit", *ABC News* (22 November 2016), www.abc.net.au/news/2016-11-23/what-robinson-crusoe-can-teach-us-about-brexit/8041656.

22 Andrew Lambert, "Preface" to *Crusoe's Island: A Rich and Curious History of Pirates, Castaways and Madness* (London: Faber and Faber, 2016).

23 Robert Clark, "Robinsonade and Brexit: Free Trade, Empire and the Whole World", in *300 Years of Robinsonades*, ed. Emmanuelle Peraldo (Newcastle: Cambridge Scholars, 2020), 165–189.

24 Clark, "Robinsonade and Brexit", 169–170.

25 Susan Naramore Maher, "Recasting Crusoe: Frederick Marryat, R.M. Ballantyne and the Nineteenth-Century Robinsonade", *Children's Literature Association Quarterly* 13.4 (1988): 169.

26 Steve Bell, "European Raft", *Belltoons* (2016), https://belltoons.co.uk/bell works/index.php/leaders/2016/4006-230616_EUROPEANRAFT.

27 *Charlie Hebdo* 1249 (29 June 2016).

28 *Evening Standard* (4 April 2019; 28 May 2019), available at Christian Adams official Twitter account: https://twitter.com/Adamstoon1/status/1113748458903 674881/photo/1 and https://twitter.com/Adamstoon1/status/1133320156585893 889/photo/1.

29 See Philip Stephens, "Boris Johnson is Wrong. Parliament Has the Ultimate Authority", *Financial Times* (25 February 2016), www.ft.com/content/ 26b6a12c-daf2-11e5-a72f-1e7744c66818.

30 See, for example, Ian Kinane, *Theorising Literary Islands: The Island Trope in Contemporary Robinsonade Narratives* (London: Rowman and Littlefield International, 2017), 103–106 and Adrian Kempton, *The Mind's Isle: Imaginary Islands in English Fiction* (Frankfurt: Peter Lang, 2017) for criticism, and Muriel Spark's island as "a place of the mind" in *Robinson* (1958; New York: New Directions Classics, 2003), 174 and the book cover of Olga Tokarczuk, *Profesor Andrews w Warszawie. Wyspa* (Warszawa: Wydawnictwo Literackie, 2018), for fiction.

31 Chloe Wigston Smith, "How Harassed Women Had Their #MeToo Moments in the 18th Century", *The Conversation* (26 February 2018), http s://theconversation.com/how-harassed-women-had-their-metoo-mom ents-in-the-18th-century-91761.

32 Thomas Lockwood, "The *Pamela* Debate", in *Prose Fiction in English from the Origins of Print to 1750*, ed. Thomas Keymer (Oxford: Oxford University Press, 2017), 555.

33 Jill Radsken, "Befriending Clarissa During Lockdown", *The Harvard Gazette* (23 September 2020), https://news.harvard.edu/gazette/story/2020/ 09/clarissa-brings-together-faculty-from-around-the-world.

34 See, for example, Lockwood, "The *Pamela* Debate", 551.

35 Rowan Pelling, "Rediscovering *Pamela*: The 1740s Blockbuster That Is Pure #MeToo", *The Telegraph* (17 January 2019), www.telegraph.co.uk/ books/what-to-read/rediscovering-pamela-1740-blockbuster-pure-metoo.

36 John Mullan, "Pamela's Power: The Novel Behind Cate Blanchett's Controversial New Play", *The Guardian* (25 January 2019), www.theguardian. com/books/2019/jan/25/pamelas-power-the-novel-behind-cate-blanchetts-controversial-new-play.

37 For a study of how *Pamela* can energise the MeToo movement itself, see Diana Rosenberger, "Virtual Rewarded: What #MeToo Can Learn from Samuel Richardson's *Pamela*", *South Central Review* 36.2 (2019): 17–32; to read on how to teach *Pamela* in the MeToo era, see Leah Grisham, "'Yield it up cheerfully': Teaching Consent, Violence, and Coercion in Samuel

Richardson's *Pamela*", *ABO: Interactive Journal for Women in the Arts, 1640–1830* 10.2 (2020), https://scholarcommons.usf.edu/abo/vol10/iss2/5.

38 Jonathan Sachs, "The Future of the Eighteenth Century", *The Rambling* 9 (2020), https://the-rambling.com/2020/08/07/issue9-sachs.

39 Lola Olufemi, "'We Can Enact the Future We Want Now': A Black Feminist History of Abolition", *The Guardian* (3 August 2020), www.theguardian.com/books/2020/aug/03/we-can-enact-the-future-we-want-now-a-black-feminist-history-of-abolition.

40 Mark Bridge, "Black Lives Matter: Plaque Review May Question Monty's Views on African 'Savages'", *The Times* (15 June 2020), www.thetimes.co.uk/article/black-lives-matter-plaque-review-may-question-monty-s-views-on-african-savages-72wchr5zh.

41 See S.E. Ogude, "Facts into Fiction: Equiano's Narrative Reconsidered", *Research in African Literatures* 13.1 (1982): 31–43.

42 "Olaudah Equiano", https://blacklivesmatter.uk/historical-contemporary-profiles/olaudah-equiano.

43 Lydia Lindsey and Carlton E. Wilson, "Reinventing European History to Show that Black Lives Do Matter", *EuropeNow: A Journal of Research and Art* (5 April 2019), www.europenowjournal.org/2019/04/04/reinventing-european-history-to-show-that-black-lives-do-matter.

44 Catherine Pepinster, "Daniel Defoe's *Journal of the Plague Year* Reprinted After Selling Out", *The Telegraph* (21 March 2020), www.telegraph.co.uk/news/2020/03/21/daniel-defoes-journal-plague-year-reprinted-selling.

45 See, for example, Jane Ciabattari, "The Plague Writers Who Predicted Today", *BBC Culture* (14 April 2020), www.bbc.com/culture/article/20200413-what-can-we-learn-from-pandemic-fiction.

46 Daniel Cook and Nicholas Seager, "Introduction", in *The Afterlives of Eighteenth-Century Fiction*, ed. Daniel Cook and Nicholas Seager (Cambridge: Cambridge University Press, 2015), 5.

Bibliography

A Catalogue of Prints and Books of Prints. London: Hooper and Davis, 1780.

Allingham, Philip V. "Thomas Stothard's Robinson Crusoe and Friday making a tent to lodge Friday's father and the Spaniard". The Victorian Web. 2018, www.victorianweb.org/art/illustration/stothard/19.html.

Aleksandrowicz, Alina. "Nieznana 'Podróż sentymentalna' Marii Wirtemberskiej". *Pamiętnik Literacki* 59. 2 (1968): 5–39.

Aleksandrowicz, Alina. *Izabela Czartoryska: Polskość i europejskość*. Lublin: Wydawnictwo Uniwersytetu Marii Curie-Skłodowskiej, 1998.

Aleksandrowicz-Ulrich, Alina. "Nieznana 'podróż' sentymentalna Marii Wirtemberskiej". *Pamiętnik Literacki* 59. 2 (1968): 5–39.

Asfour, Lana. *Laurence Sterne in France*. London: Continuum, 2008.

Bainbridge, Simon (ed.). *Romanticism: A Sourcebook*. Houndmills: Palgrave Macmillan, 2008.

Baine, Rodney M. "The Evidence from Defoe's Title Pages". *Studies in Bibliography* 25 (1972): 185–191.

Barchas, Janine. *Graphic Design, Print Culture, and the Eighteenth-Century Novel*. Cambridge: Cambridge University Press, 2003.

Bartoszyński, Kazimierz. "Sternizm". In *Słownik literatury polskiego oświecenia*. Ed. Teresa Kostkiewiczowa. Wrocław: Ossolineum, 2002.

Bates, Robin. "If Trump Tweeted Classic Lit Reviews...". *Better Living through Beowulf*. 16 March 2016. https://betterlivingthroughbeowulf.com/imagining-trump-as-a-lit-critic.

Batten, Charles L. Jr. *Pleasurable Instruction: Form and Convention in Eighteenth-Century Travel Literature*. Berkeley: University of California Press, 1978.

Battestin, Martin C. *The Providence of Wit: Aspects of Form in Augustan Literature and the Arts*. Oxford: Clarendon Press, 1974.

Battestin, Martin C. *A Henry Fielding Companion*. Westport and London: Greenwood Press, 2000.

Baudrillard, Jean. *Simulacra and Simulation*. 1981. Trans. Sheila Faria Glaser. Ann Arbor: University of Michigan Press, 2008.

Bell, Steve. "European Raft". *Belltoons.* 2016. https://belltoons.co.uk/bellworks/index.php/leaders/2016/4006-230616_EUROPEANRAFT.

Bellhouse, Mary L. "On Understanding Rousseau's Praise of Robinson Crusoe". *Canadian Journal of Social and Political Theory/Revue canadienne de theorie politique et sociale* 6. 3 (1982): 120–137.

Blaim, Artur. *Robinson Crusoe and His Doubles: The English Robinsonade of the Eighteenth Century.* Frankfurt: Peter Lang, 2016.

Blanton, Casey. *Travel Writing: The Self and the World.* London and New York: Routledge, 2002.

Blewett, David. *The Illustration of Robinson Crusoe, 1719–1920.* Gerrards Cross: Smythe, 1995.

Blewett, David. "The Iconic Crusoe: Illustrations and Images of Robinson Crusoe." In *The Cambridge Companion to Robinson Crusoe.* Ed. John Richetti. Cambridge: Cambridge University Press, 2018. 159–190.

Bohuszewicz, Paweł. *Od "romansu" do powieści: Studia o polskiej literaturze narracyjnej (druga połowa XVII wieku – pierwsza połowa XIX wieku).* Toruń: Wydawnictwo Naukowe Uniwersytetu Mikołaja Kopernika, 2016.

Brewer, David A. *The Afterlife of Character, 1726–1825.* Philadelphia: University of Pennsylvania Press, 2005.

Bridge, Mark. "Black Lives Matter: Plaque Review May Question Monty's Views on African 'Savages'". *The Times.* 15 June 2020. www.thetimes.co.uk/article/black-lives-matter-plaque-review-may-question-monty-s-views-on-african-savages-72wchr5zh.

Brown, Homer Obed. "The Institution of the English Novel: Defoe's Contribution". *Novel: A Forum on Fiction* 29. 3 (1996): 299–318.

Burney, Frances. *Evelina.* Ed. Edward A. Bloom, intr. and notes Vivien Jones. Oxford: Oxford University Press, 2008.

Butterwick, Richard. *Poland's Last King and English Culture: Stanisław August Poniatowski, 1732–1798.* Oxford: Clarendon, 1998.

Bystydzieńska, Grażyna. "Wawrzyniec Sterne: A Sentimental Journey in 19th Century Poland". *The Shandean* 13 (2002): 47–53.

Bystydzieńska, Grażyna. "O polskich przekładach literatury angielskiej w XVIII wieku". *Wiek Oświecenia* 29 (2013): 99–112.

Bystydzieńska, Grażyna and Wojciech Nowicki. "Sterne in Poland". In *The Reception of Laurence Sterne in Europe.* Ed. Peter de Voogd and John Neubauer. London: Continuum, 2004. 154–164.

Carlson, Michael. "Brexit: A Modest Proposal". *ARC.* 8 October 2019. https://arcdigital.media/brexit-a-modest-proposal-124e47ec6c1e.

Charlie Hebdo 1249. 29 June 2016.

Ciabattari, Jane. "The Plague Writers Who Predicted Today". *BBC Culture.* 14 April 2020. www.bbc.com/culture/article/20200413-what-can-we-learn-from-pandemic-fiction.

Clark, Robert. "Robinsonade and Brexit: Free Trade, Empire and the Whole World". In *300 Years of Robinsonades.* Ed. Emmanuelle Peraldo. Newcastle: Cambridge Scholars, 2020. 165–189.

Coetzee, J.M. *Foe*. London: Penguin Books, 1987.

Coleridge, Samuel Taylor. *Collected Letters of Samuel Taylor Coleridge*. Ed. Earl Leslie Griggs. Vol. 5. Oxford: Clarendon Press, 1971.

Cook, Daniel. "Authors Unformed: Reading 'Beauties' in the Eighteenth Century". *Philological Quarterly* 89. 2–3 (2010): 283–309.

Cook, Daniel. "On Authorship, Appropriation, and Eighteenth-Century Fiction". In *The Afterlives of Eighteenth-Century Fiction*. Ed. Daniel Cook and Nicholas Seager. Cambridge: Cambridge University Press, 2015. 20–42.

Cook, Daniel and Nicholas Seager (eds.). *The Afterlives of Eighteenth-Century Fiction*. Cambridge: Cambridge University Press, 2015.

Cook, Daniel and Nicholas Seager. "Introduction". In *The Afterlives of Eighteenth-Century Fiction*. Ed. Daniel Cook and Nicholas Seager. Cambridge: Cambridge University Press, 2015. 1–19.

Curley, Thomas M. *Sterne's All Before Them, 1660–1780*. Ed. John McVeagh. London and Atlantic Highlands, NJ: The Ashfield Press, 1990. 203–216.

Czartoryska, Izabela. *Dyliżansem przez Śląsk: Dziennik podróży do Cieplic w roku 1816*. Wrocław: Zakład Narodowy im. Ossolińskich, 1968.

Czartoryska, Izabela. *Extraits*. 3 vols. The Czartoryski Library in Cracow. MS 6070.

Czartoryska, Izabela. *Katalog pamiątek złożonych w Domu Gotyckim w Puławach*. The Czartoryski Library in Cracow. MS 2917.

Czartoryska, Izabela. Letter to her daughter Mary from 5 February 1784. The Czartoryski Library in Cracow. MS 6137 II.

Czartoryska, Izabela. Letter to her husband Adam Kazimierz from 3 July 1811. The Czartoryski Library in Cracow. MS 6030 III.

Dąbrowicz, Elżbieta. "Syndrom rozbitka. Robinson Crusoe i Julian Ursyn Niemcewicz". *Porównania* 25. 2 (2019): 21–42.

Dąbrowska, Magdalena. *Dla pożytku i przyjemności: Rosyjska podróż sentymentalna przełomu XVIII i XIX wieku*. Warszawa: Wydawnictwa Uniwersytetu Warszawskiego, 2009.

Dąbrowska, Magdalena. "W stronę instrukcji. Listy z Londynu Piotra Makarowa w kontekście dyskusji nad gatunkiem podróży sentymentalnej w czasopismach rosyjskich początku XIX wieku". In *Metamorfozy podróży: Kultura i tożsamość*. Ed. Jolanta Sztachelska *et al*. Białystok: Wydawnictwo Uniwersytetu w Białymstoku, 2012.

[Defoe, Daniel]. *Przypadki Robinsona Krusoe*. Trans. Jan Chrzciciel Albertrandi. Warszawa: Nakładem Michała Grela, 1769.

Defoe, Daniel. *A Tour Thro' the Whole Island of Great Britain*, volume I. Ed. John McVeagh. *Writings on Travel, Discovery and History*. Ed. W. R. Owens and P. N. Furbank. Vol. 1. London: Pickering and Chatto, 2001–2002.

Defoe, Daniel. *The Life and Strange Surprising Adventures of Robinson Crusoe (1719)*. *The Novels of Daniel Defoe*. Ed. W. R. Owens and P. N. Furbank. Vol. 1. London: Pickering & Chatto, 2008.

Defoe, Daniel. *The Farther Adventures of Robinson Crusoe*. Ed. W. R. Owens. London: Routledge, 2017.

Doody, Margaret Anne. *The True History of the Novel*. New Brunswick, NJ: Rutgers University Press, 1996.

"Editions in French and Some Other Translations". In *Robinson Crusoe at Yale*. *Yale University Library Gazette* 11. 2 (1936): 28–32.

Evening Standard, 4 April 2019; 28 May 2019.

Fanning, Christopher. "Small Particles of Eloquence: Sterne and the Scriblerian Text". *Modern Philology* 100. 3 (2003): 360–392.

Feliński, Alojzy. *Ziemianin, czyli ziemiaństwo francuskie Jakuba Delille'a przez Alojzego Felińskiego wierszem polskim przełożone*. Kraków, 1823.

Fielding, Henry. *The History and Adventures of Joseph Andrews*. Ed. Martin C. Battestin. Middletown, CT: Wesleyan University Press, 1967.

Fielding, Henry. *A Journey from this World to the Next*. Ed. Claude Rawson. London: Dent, 1973.

Fielding, Henry. *The History of Tom Jones, A Foundling*. Ed. Martin C. Battestin and Fredson Bowers. Middletown: Wesleyan University Press, 1975.

Fitzpatrick, Martin and Peter Jones (eds.). *The Reception of Edmund Burke in Europe*. London: Bloomsbury, 2017.

Garrison, Alyssia. "Those Naked Donald Trump Statues? They Have a Secret History". *The National Book Review*. 2 November 2016. www.thenationalbookreview.com/features/2016/11/2/essay-those-naked-donald-trump-statues-they-have-a-secret-history.

Garrison, Ben. "The Sleeping Giant Finally Wakes Up". 2013. https://grrrgraphics.com/sleeping-giant-finally-wakes-up.

Gevirtz, Karen Bloom. *Representing the Eighteenth-Century in Film and Television, 2000–2015*. Houndmills: Palgrave Macmillan, 2017.

Genette, Gérard. *The Architext: An Introduction*. Berkeley: University of California Press, 1992.

Genette, Gérard. *Palimpsests: Literature in the Second Degree*. Trans. Channa Newman and Claude Doubinsky. Lincoln and London: University of Nebraska Press, 1997.

Genette, Gérard. *Paratexts: Thresholds of Interpretation*. Trans. Jane E. Lewin. Cambridge: Cambridge University Press, 1997.

Ghent, Dorothy van. *The English Novel: Form and Function*. New York: Rhinehart, 1953.

Gibson, William L. *Art and Money in the Writings of Tobias Smollett*. Lewisburg: Bucknell University Press, 2007.

Gołębiowska, Zofia. *W kręgu Czartoryskich: Wpływy angielskie w Puławach na przełomie XVIII i XIX wieku*. Lublin: Wydawnictwo Uniwersytetu Marii Curie-Skłodowskiej, 2000.

Gołębiowska, Zofia. "British Models and Inspirations in Czartoryskis' Country Residence in Puławy at the Turn of the Eighteenth Century". In *Culture at Global/ Local Levels: British and Commonwealth Contribution to World Civilisation*. Ed. Krystyna Kujawińska-Courtney. Łódź: Wydawnictwo Biblioteka, 2002. 139–150.

Gottlieb, Evan. *Engagements with Contemporary Literary and Critical Theory*. London and New York: Routledge, 2020.

Gordon, Catherine M. *British Paintings of Subjects from the English Novel, 1740–1870.* New York: Garland, 1988.

Graciotti, Sante and Jadwiga Rudnicka (eds.). *Inwentarz biblioteki Ignacego Krasickiego z 1810 r.* Wrocław: Zakład Narodowy im. Ossolińskich, 1973.

Grisham, Leah. "'Yield it up cheerfully': Teaching Consent, Violence, and Coercion in Samuel Richardson's *Pamela*". *ABO: Interactive Journal for Women in the Arts, 1640–1830* 10. 2 (2020). https://scholarcommons.usf.edu/abo/vol10/iss2/5.

Groom, Gloria. "Art, Illustration, and Enterprise in Late Eighteenth-Century English Art: A Painting by Philippe Jacques de Loutherbourg". *Art Institute of Chicago Museum Studies* 18. 2 (1992): 124–135.

Hagstrum, Jean H. *The Sister Arts: The Tradition of Literary Pictorialism and English Poetry from Dryden to Gray.* Chicago: University of Chicago Press, 1958.

Hilles, Frederick. "Art and Artifice". In *Imagined Worlds: Essays on Some English Novels and Novelists in Honour of John Butt.* Ed. Maynard Mack and Ian Gregor. London: Methuen, 1968. 91–110.

Hogarth, William. *The Analysis of Beauty.* Ed. Ronald Paulson. New Haven and London: Yale University Press, 1997.

Hogle, Jerrold E. "The Ghost of the Counterfeit in the Genesis of the Gothic". In *Gothic Origins and Innovations.* Ed. Allan Lloyd Smith and Victor Sage. Amsterdam and Atlanta: Rodopi, 1994. 23–33.

Holland, Anna and Richard Scholar (eds.). *Pre-Histories and Afterlives: Studies in Critical Method for Terence Cave.* London: Legenda, 2009.

"How The Handmaid's Tale Costumes in Protests Impact Political Change". *CBC News: The National.* YouTube, 7 June 2019. www.youtube.com/watch?v=bxPaX79U6RI.

Ionescu, Christina and Ann Lewis (eds.). Special Issue: Picturing the Eighteenth-Century Novel through Time: Illustration, Intermediality and Adaptation. *Journal for Eighteenth-Century Studies* 39. 4 (2016).

Iser, Wolfgang. *The Act of Reading: A Theory of Aesthetic Response.* London: Routledge & Kegan Paul, 1978.

Jackson, Spencer. *We Are Kings: Political Theology and the Making of a Modern Individual.* Charlottesville: University of Virginia Press, 2020.

Jauss, Hans Robert. *Toward an Aesthetic of Reception.* Minneapolis: University of Minnesota Press, 1982.

Journal Polonais 3 (1769).

Juda, Maria. "Uprzywilejowane drukarnie we Lwowie doby staropolskiej". *Folia Bibliologica* 55/56 (2013/2014): 11–18.

Kalinowska, Izabela. *Between East and West: Polish and Russian Nineteenth-Century Travel to the Orient.* Rochester, NY: University of Rochester Press, 2004.

Keenan, Brendan. "View from Dublin: What Jonathan Swift Would Say about Brexit". *Belfast Telegraph.* 16 April 2019. www.belfasttelegraph.co.uk/business/analysis/view-from-dublin-what-jonathan-swift-would-say-about-brexit-38014353.html.

Kefferpütz, Roderick. "Trumping Trump: A Gulliver Strategy". *Medium*. 6 July 2017. https://medium.com/everyvote/trumping-trump-a-gulliver-strategy-3fc96 e4d5d93.

Kempton, Adrian. *The Mind's Isle: Imaginary Islands in English Fiction*. Frankfurt: Peter Lang, 2017.

Keogh, Laurence. "A City of Words: Jonathan Swift". *Dublin: Official Site for News, Information and Events*. 2017. https://dublin.ie/live/stories/city-of-words-jonathan-swift.

Keymer, Thomas. *Sterne, the Moderns, and the Novel*. Oxford: Oxford University Press, 2002.

Kinane, Ian. *Theorising Literary Islands: The Island Trope in Contemporary Robinsonade Narratives*. London and New York: Rowman & Littlefield International, 2017.

Kinane, Ian (ed.). *Didactics and the Modern Robinsonade*. Liverpool: Liverpool University Press, 2019.

Klimowicz, Mieczysław. "Wstęp". In *Ignacy Krasicki. Mikołaja Doświadczyńskiego przypadki*. Ed. Mieczysław Klimowicz. Wrocław: Zakład Narodowy im. Ossolińskich, 1975. iii-lxi.

Korte, Barbara. *English Travel Writing: From Pilgrimages to Postcolonial Explorations*. Trans. Catherine Matthias. London: Macmillan, 2000.

Kott, Jan. *Shakespeare Our Contemporary*. Trans. Bolesław Taborski. New York: Double Day, 1964.

Krasicki, Ignacy. *Mikołaja Doświadczyńskiego przypadki*. Ed. Mieczysław Klimowicz. Wrocław: Zakład Narodowy im. Ossolińskich, 1975.

Krasicki, Ignacy. *The Adventures of Mr. Nicholas Wisdom*. Trans. Thomas H. Hoisington. Evanston, IL: Northwestern University Press, 1992.

Krasicki, Ignacy. *Historia*. Kraków: Universitas, 2002.

Kurządkowska, Beata. "Między rzeczywistością a fikcją w relacji z podróży Marii Wirtemberskiej 'Niektóre zdarzenia, myśli i uczucia doznane za granicą'". *Prace Literaturoznawcze* 1 (2013): 35-45.

Lambert, Andrew. *Crusoe's Island: A Rich and Curious History of Pirates, Castaways and Madness*. London: Faber and Faber, 2016.

Lambert, Andrew. "What Robinson Crusoe Can Teach Us about Brexit". *ABC News*. 22 November 2016. www.abc.net.au/news/2016-11-23/what-robinson-crusoe-can-teach-us-about-brexit/8041656.

Lindfield, Peter N. "Imagining the Undefined Castle in The Castle of Otranto: Engravings and Interpretations". *Image [&] Narrative* 18. 3 (2017): 46-63.

Lindsey, Lydia and Carlton E.Wilson. "Reinventing European History to Show that Black Lives Do Matter". *EuropeNow: A Journal of Research and Art*. 5 April 2019. www.europenowjournal.org/2019/04/04/reinventing-europ ean-history-to-show-that-black-lives-do-matter.

Lipski, Jakub. *In Quest of the Self: Masquerade and Travel in the Eighteenth-Century Novel. Fielding, Smollett, Sterne*. Amsterdam and New York: Rodopi, 2014.

Lipski, Jakub (ed.). *Rewriting Crusoe: The Robinsonade across Languages, Cultures, and Media*. Lewisburg: Bucknell University Press, 2020.

Lockwood, Thomas. *Prose Fiction in English from the Origins of Print to 1750*. Ed. Thomas Keymer. Oxford: Oxford University Press, 2017. 548–562.

Longueville, Peter. *The Hermit, or, the Unparalled Sufferings and Surprising Adventures of Mr Philip Quarll, an Englishman*. London: Printed by J. Cluer and A. Campbell, 1727.

Maher, Susan Naramore. "Recasting Crusoe: Frederick Marryat, R.M. Ballantyne and the Nineteenth-Century Robinsonade". *Children's Literature Association Quarterly* 13. 4 (1988): 169–175.

Mandal, Anthony and Brian Southam (eds.). *The Reception of Jane Austen in Europe*. London: Continuum, 2007.

Marzec, Robert. *An Ecological and Postcolonial Study of Literature: from Daniel Defoe to Salman Rushdie*. New York: Palgrave, 2007.

Mayer, Robert (ed.). *Eighteenth-Century Fiction on Screen*. Cambridge: Cambridge University Press, 2002.

McCreedy, Jonathan, Vesselin M.Budakov and Alexandra K.Glavanakova (eds.). *Swiftian Inspirations: The Legacy of Jonathan Swift from the Enlightenment to the Age of Post-Truth*. Newcastle: Cambridge Scholars, 2020.

McCreedy, Jonathan. "Is Brexit the Modern-Day 'Wood's Halfpence'? Re-Evaluating Swift's Economic Policies in a Time of Contemporary Crisis and Uncertainty in Ireland". In *Swiftian Inspirations: The Legacy of Jonathan Swift from the Enlightenment to the Age of Post-Truth*. Ed. Jonathan McCreedy, Vesselin M. Budakov and Alexandra K. Glavanakova. Newcastle: Cambridge Scholars, 2020. 225–246.

Meer, Jan IJ. van der. *Literary Activities and Attitudes in the Stanislavian Age in Poland (1764–1795): A Social System?* Amsterdam: Rodopi, 2002.

Michals, Teresa. *Books for Children, Books for Adults: Age and the Novel from Defoe to James*. Cambridge: Cambridge University Press, 2014.

Miłosz, Czesław. *The History of Polish Literature*. Berkeley: University of California Press, 1983.

Montaigne, Michel de. *The Complete Essays of Montaigne*. Stanford, CA: Stanford University Press, 1958.

Moroz, Grzegorz. *Travellers, Novelists and Gentlemen: Constructing Male Narrative Personae in British Travel Books, from the Beginnings to the Second World War*. Frankfurt am Main: Peter Lang, 2013.

Moszyński, August Fryderyk. *Rozprawa o ogrodnictwie angielskim, 1774*. Ed. Agnieszka Morawińska. Wrocław: Zakład Narodowy im. Ossolińskich, 1977.

Mueller, Andreas K. E. and Glynis Ridley (eds.). *Robinson Crusoe after 300 Years*. Lewisburg: Bucknell University Press, 2021.

Mullan, John. "Pamela's Power: The Novel Behind Cate Blanchett's Controversial New Play". *The Guardian*. 25 January 2019. www.theguardian.com/books/2019/jan/25/pamelas-power-the-novel-behind-cate-blanchetts-controversial-new-play.

Newbould, M.-C. *Adaptations of Laurence Sterne's Fiction: Sterneana, 1760–1840*. Aldershot and Burlington: Ashgate, 2013.

Newbould, M-C. "Wit and Humour for the Heart of Sensibility: The Beauties of Fielding and Sterne". In *The Afterlives of Eighteenth-Century Fiction*. Ed.

Daniel Cook and Nicholas Seager. Cambridge: Cambridge University Press, 2015. 133–152.

Novak, Maximillian E. *Transformations, Ideology, and the Real in Defoe's Robinson Crusoe and Other Narratives: Finding "The Thing Itself"*. Newark: University of Delaware Press, 2015.

Nowicki, Wojciech. "An Anachronistic Hoax". *The Shandean* 13 (2002): 106–109.

Ogude, S.E. "Facts into Fiction: Equiano's Narrative Reconsidered". *Research in African Literatures* 13. 1 (1982): 31–43.

"Olaudah   Equiano".   https://blacklivesmatter.uk/historical-contemporary-p rofiles/olaudah-equiano.

Olufemi, Lola. "'We Can Enact the Future We Want Now': A Black Feminist History of Abolition". *The Guardian*. 3 August 2020. www.theguardian.com/books/ 2020/aug/03/we-can-enact-the-future-we-want-now-a-black-feminist-history-of-a bolition.

Ożarska, Magdalena. *Two Women Writers and their Italian Tours: Mary Shelley's Rambles in Germany and Italy and Łucja Rautenstrauchowa's In and Beyond the Alps*. Lewiston, NY: The Edwin Mellen Press, 2013.

Ożarska, Magdalena. "A Striking Reduction of the Visual: The Imaginative and the Familial Gaze in Maria Wirtemberska's Niektóre zdarzenia, myśli i uczucia doznane za granicą [Certain events, thoughts and feelings experienced abroad] (1816–1818)". *Studies in Travel Writing* 22. 1 (2018): 59–76.

Paley, Morton D. and Sibylle Erle (eds.). *The Reception of William Blake in Europe*. London: Bloomsbury, 2019.

Parnell, Tim. "*The Sermons of Mr. Yorick*: The Commonplace and the Rhetoric of the Heart". In *The Cambridge Companion to Laurence Sterne*. Ed. Thomas Keymer. Cambridge: Cambridge University Press, 2009. 64–77.

Patten, Robert L. *George Cruikshank's Life, Times, and Art. Volume 1: 1792– 1835*. New Brunswick: Rutgers University Press, 1992.

Paulson, Ronald. "Putting out the Fire in Her Imperial Majesty's Apartment: Opposition Politics, Anticlericalism, and Aesthetics". *ELH* 63. 1 (1996): 79–107.

Pelling, Rowan. "Rediscovering *Pamela*: The 1740s Blockbuster That Is Pure #MeToo". *The Telegraph*. 17 January 2019. www.telegraph.co.uk/books/ what-to-read/rediscovering-pamela-1740-blockbuster-pure-metoo.

Pepinster, Catherine. "Daniel Defoe's *Journal of the Plague Year* Reprinted After Selling Out". *The Telegraph*. 21 March 2020. www.telegraph.co.uk/ news/2020/03/21/daniel-defoes-journal-plague-year-reprinted-selling.

Peraldo, Emmanuelle (ed.). *300 Years of Robinsonades*. Newcastle: Cambridge Scholars, 2020.

Pulte, Helmut and Scott Mandelbrote (eds.). *The Reception of Isaac Newton in Europe*. London: Bloomsbury, 2019.

Punter, David and Glennis Byron. *The Gothic*. Oxford: Blackwell, 2004.

Radcliffe, Ann. *The Italian*. Ed. E.J. Clery. Oxford: Oxford University Press, 2008.

Radsken, Jill. "Befriending Clarissa During Lockdown". *The Harvard Gazette*. 23 September 2020. https://news.harvard.edu/gazette/story/2020/09/clarissa-brings-together-faculty-from-around-the-world.

Rawson, Claude Julien. *Henry Fielding and the Augustan Ideal under Stress: "Nature's Dances of Death" and Other Studies.* London and Boston: Routledge and Kegan Paul, 1972.

Rawson, Claude. *Gulliver and the Gentle Reader: Studies in Swift and Our Time.* London: Routledge and Kegan Paul, 1973.

Real, Hermann J. (ed.). *The Reception of Jonathan Swift in Europe.* London: Continuum, 2005.

Rezmer-Mrówczyńska, Natalia. "Sterne in Poland in the Age of the Enlightenment". *The Shandean* 24 (2013): 117–126.

Rigney, Ann. *The Afterlives of Walter Scott: Memory on the Move.* Oxford: Oxford University Press, 2012.

Robertson, Scott. *Henry Fielding: Literary and Theological Misplacement.* Bern: Peter Lang, 2010.

Rosenberger, Diana. "Virtual Rewarded: What #MeToo Can Learn from Samuel Richardson's Pamela". *South Central Review* 36. 2 (2019): 17–32.

Rousseau, Jean-Jacques. *The Reveries of a Solitary.* Trans. John Gould Fletcher. New York: Burt Franklin, 1971.

Rousseau, Jean-Jacques. "Julie, or the New Heloise". In *The Collected Writings of Rousseau.* Vol. 6. Trans. Philip Stewart and Jean Vache. Hanover, NH: University Press of New England, 1997.

Rousseau, Jean-Jacques. *Emile, or On Education.* Ed. and trans. Christopher Kelly and Allan Bloom. Hanover, NH: University Press of New England, 2010.

Rowson, Martin. *The Life and Opinions of Tristram Shandy.* London: Picador, 1996.

Rowson, Martin. *Gulliver's Travels.* London: Atlantic Books, 2012.

Rudnicka, Jadwiga (ed.). *Biblioteka Stanisława Augusta na Zamku Warszawskim: Dokumenty, Archiwum Literackie* 26 (1988): 67–83.

Ruszała, Jadwiga. *Robinson w literaturze polskiej.* Słupsk: Wydawnictwo Wyższej Szkoły Pedagogicznej w Słupsku, 1998.

Ruszała, Jadwiga. *Robinsonada w literaturze polskiej.* Słupsk: Wydawnictwo Akademii Pomorskiej w Słupsku, 2000.

Sachs, Jonathan. "The Future of the Eighteenth Century". *The Rambling* 9 (2020). https://the-rambling.com/2020/08/07/issue9-sachs.

Sharp, Samuel. *Letters from Italy.* London: Printed for R. Cave, 1767.

Simonova, Natasha. *Early Modern Authorship and Prose Continuations: Adaptation and Ownership from Sidney to Richardson.* Houndmills: Palgrave Macmillan, 2015.

Sinko, Zofia. *Powieść angielska osiemnastego wieku a powieść polska lat, 1764–1830.* Warszawa: Państwowy Instytut Wydawniczy, 1961.

Sinko, Zofia. "Powieść zachodnioeuropejska w Polsce stanisławowskiej na podstawie inwentarzy bibliotecznych i katalogów". *Pamiętnik Literacki* 57. 4 (1966): 581–624.

Sinko, Zofia. *Powieść zachodnioeuropejska w kulturze literackiej polskiego Oświecenia.* Wrocław: Zakład Narodowy im. Ossolińskich, 1968.

Smallman, Etan. An Interview with Michael Morpurgo: Michael Morpurgo on Fighting Brexit: 'I've been spat at. It's almost civil war'. *The Guardian.*

13 September 2019. www.theguardian.com/books/2019/sep/13/michael-morp urgo-boy-giant-brexit-refugee-crisis-trump-civil-war.

Smith, Chloe Wigston. "How Harassed Women Had Their #MeToo Moments in the 18th Century". *The Conversation*. 26 February 2018. https://theconversation. com/how-harassed-women-had-their-metoo-moments-in-the-18th-century-91761.

Smollett, Tobias. *Travels through France and Italy*. Fwd. Ted Jones, intr. Thomas Seccombe. New York: Tauris Parke, 2010.

Spark, Muriel. *Robinson*. 1958. New York: New Directions Classics, 2003.

Spencer, Jane. *Aphra Behn's Afterlife*. Oxford: Oxford University Press, 2000.

Stein, Perrin and Mary Tavener Holmes, *Eighteenth-Century French Drawings in New York Collections*. New York: The Metropolitan Museum of Art, 1999, 164.

Stephens, Philip. "Boris Johnson is Wrong. Parliament Has the Ultimate Authority". *Financial Times*. 25 February 2016. www.ft.com/content/26b6a 12c-daf2-11e5-a72f-1e7744c66818.

Sterne, Laurence. *Suite de la Vie et des opinions de Tristram Shandy*. Trans. Charles-François de Bonnay. Paris: Volland, 1785.

Sterne, Laurence. *The Sermons of Laurence Sterne*. Ed. Melvyn New. Gaines-ville, FL: University Press of Florida, 1996.

Sterne, Laurence. *A Sentimental Journey through France and Italy and Con-tinuation of the Bramine's Journal*. Ed. Melvyn New and W.G. Day. Gains-ville, FL: University Press of Florida, 2002.

Sterne, Laurence. *The Letters*. Ed. Melvyn New and Peter de Voogd. Gaines-ville, FL: University Press of Florida, 2009.

Sterne, Laurence. *A Sentimental Journey*. Ed. Patrick Wildgust and Helen Williams. Coxwold: Shandy Hall Press, 2018.

Stevenson, John Allen. "*Tom Jones*, Jacobitism, and the Rise of Gothic". In *Gothic Origins and Innovations*. Ed. Allan Lloyd Smith and Victor Sage. Amsterdam and Atlanta: Rodopi, 1994. 16–22.

Stewart, Philip. *Engraven Desire: Eros, Image & Text in the French Eighteenth Century*. Durham and London: Duke University Press, 1992.

Szyrma, Krystyn Lach. *Anglia i Szkocja: Przypomnienie z podróży roku 1820–1824 odbytej*. Ed. Paweł Hertz. Warszawa: Państwowy Instytut Wydawniczy, 1981.

Taylor, David Francis. *The Politics of Parody: A Literary History of Car-icature, 1760–1830*. New Haven: Yale University Press, 2018.

Taylor-Terlecka, Nina. "Ossian in Poland". In *The Reception of Ossian in Europe*. Ed. Howard Gaskill. London: Continuum, 2004. 240–258.

The Beauties of Fielding: Carefully Selected from the Works of that Eminent Writer. To which is added Some Account of his Life. London: G. Kearsley, 1782.

Thompson, Carl. *Travel Writing*. London and New York: Routledge, 2011.

Thompson, C.W. *French Romantic Travel Writing: Chateaubriand to Nerval*. Oxford: Oxford University Press, 2012.

Tokarczuk, Olga. *Profesor Andrews w Warszawie. Wyspa*. Warszawa: Wydaw-nictwo Literackie, 2018.

Vallely, Paul. "Paul Vallely on Brexit and Ireland: A Swiftian Solution". *Church Times.* 19 October 2018. www.churchtimes.co.uk/articles/2018/19-october/comment/columnists/paul-vallely-on-brexit-and-ireland-a-swiftian-solution.

Vickers, Ilse. *Defoe and the New Sciences.* Cambridge: Cambridge University Press, 1996.

Vieweg, Klaus, James Vigus and Kathleen M.Wheeler (eds.). *Shandean Humour in English and German Literature and Philosophy.* Oxford: Legenda, 2017.

Voogd, Peter de and John Neubauer (eds.). *The Reception of Laurence Sterne in Europe.* London: Continuum, 2004.

Voogd, Peter de. "Laurence Sterne and the 'Gutter of Time'". In *Studies in English Literature and Culture: Festschrift in Honour of Professor Grażyna Bystydzieńska.* Ed. Anna Kędra-Kardela, Aleksandra Kędzierska, Magdalena Pypeć. Lublin: Maria Curie-Skłodowska University Press, 2017. 271–278.

Walpole, Horace. *The Yale Edition of Horace Walpole's Correspondence.* Ed. W.S. Lewis *et al.* New Haven and London: Yale University Press, 1937–1983.

Walpole, Horace. *The Castle of Otranto.* Ed. Nick Groom. Oxford: Oxford University Press, 2014.

Watt, Ian P. *The Rise of the Novel.* 1957. Berkeley: University of California Press, 2000.

Żołądź-Strzelczyk, Dorota. "Kilka uwag o znajomości dzieła Jana Jakuba Rousseau Emil, czyli o wychowaniu w Polsce przełomu XVIII i XIX wieku". *Problemy wczesnej edukacji* 2. 29 (2015): 7–14.

Index

Printed in the United States
by Baker & Taylor Publisher Services

Printed in the United States
by Baker & Taylor Publisher Services